Introduction to Maternal Newborn Nursing Exam

The Maternal Newborn Nursing Exam stands as a preeminent assessment for nurses aspiring to showcase their specialized prowess in the multifaceted realm of maternal and newborn care. This certification constitutes a testament to a nurse's adeptness in orchestrating comprehensive care strategies that encompass the continuum from pregnancy and childbirth to postpartum and neonatal care. The rigors of this examination illuminate a candidate's profound comprehension and proficiency in navigating the intricate tapestry of challenges and opportunities inherent in this vital domain.

Outline of the Maternal Newborn Nursing Exam:

1. 175 multiple-choice questions

2. 25 unscored pretest questions for future validation

3. Time Limit: 3 hours

Content Categories

A. Pregnancy, Birth Risk Factors, and Complications (7%):

1. Antenatal factors and risk assessment

2. Intrapartum factors and complications

B. Maternal Postpartum Assessment, Management, and Education (26%):

1. Physiological changes and physical assessment

2. Nursing care strategies for maternal well-being

3. Lactation support and guidance

4. Addressing psychosocial, ethical, and family-oriented matters

5. Newborn feeding and nutritional considerations

C. Newborn Assessment and Management (19%):

1. Transition to extra uterine life

2. Comprehensive physical assessment, including gestational age evaluation

3. Family-focused newborn care and educational outreach

4. Resuscitation and stabilization techniques

D. Maternal Postpartum Complications (24%):

1. Hematologic complications in the postpartum period

2. Cardiovascular challenges and interventions

3. Infections and related management strategies

4. Diabetes and its implications

5. Mood disorders, substance use issues, and their treatment

E. Newborn Complications (24%):

1. Cardiovascular and respiratory intricacies

2. Neurological and gastrointestinal challenges

3. Hematologic anomalies and management approaches

4. Infectious diseases affecting newborns

5. Genetic, metabolic, and endocrine considerations

Mastering Maternal Newborn Nursing: Comprehensive Practice Tests

Dive into the world of maternal and newborn care with our comprehensive exam preparation book, "Mastering Maternal Newborn Nursing: Comprehensive Practice Tests." Designed specifically for nurses aiming to excel in maternal and newborn healthcare, this book offers a holistic approach to mastering the intricacies of this vital field. Whether you're a seasoned nurse seeking certification or a student eager to fortify your knowledge, this book is your ultimate companion.

Inside, you'll find a meticulously crafted resource featuring not just one, but seven full-length practice tests. Each practice test mirrors the actual Maternal Newborn Nursing Exam, allowing you to familiarize yourself with the format, question types, and time constraints. These practice tests are strategically designed to challenge your understanding and critical thinking skills across a spectrum of scenarios encountered during pregnancy, childbirth, postpartum care, and neonatal management.

Seven Comprehensive Practice Tests: Elevate your readiness with an array of practice tests that progressively build your confidence and competence.

Realistic Exam Experience: Immerse yourself in the actual testing environment. Each practice test closely replicates the exam's structure and difficulty.

GREYSCALE

BIN TRAVELER FORM

Cut By __Katiuska V #34__ Qty __38 (+7)__ Date __02/25/26__

Scanned By _____ Qty _____ Date _____

Scanned Batch ID's

Notes/Exception

Thorough Content Coverage: Encounter a rich tapestry of questions spanning antenatal factors, maternal postpartum care, newborn assessment, complications, and more.

Performance Tracking: Gauge your progress with detailed performance analysis. Identify strengths, target areas for improvement, and refine your study strategy.

Time Management Mastery: Develop your pacing skills and time management abilities, essential for acing the actual exam.

Introduction to Maternal Newborn Nursing Exam 1
    Outline of the Maternal Newborn Nursing Exam 1
    Content Categories 1

Mastering Maternal Newborn Nursing: Comprehensive Practice Tests 2
    Seven Comprehensive Practice Tests 2
    Realistic Exam Experience 2
    Thorough Content Coverage 3
    Performance Tracking 3
    Time Management Mastery 3

Maternal Newborn Nursing Exam Practice Test 1 5
    Test 1 Answer Key 38

Maternal Newborn Nursing Exam Practice Test 2 41
    Test 2 Answer Key 72

Maternal Newborn Nursing Exam Practice Test 3 75
    Test 3 Answer Key 107

Maternal Newborn Nursing Exam Practice Test 4 110
    Test 4 Answer Key 142

Maternal Newborn Nursing Exam Practice Test 5 145
    Test 5 Answer Key 178

Maternal Newborn Nursing Exam Practice Test 6 181
    Test 6 Answer Key 213

Maternal Newborn Nursing Exam Practice Test 7 216
    Test 7 Answer Key 248

Maternal Newborn Nursing Exam Practice Test 1

Q1: Which antenatal factor can contribute to a higher risk of complications during pregnancy and childbirth?

A. Advanced maternal age

B. Multiparity

C. History of previous uncomplicated pregnancies

Q2: Within 2 to 3 hours of birth, a newborn temperature should stabilize at:

A. 36.5-37°C (97.7-98.6°F)

B. 35.4-36.4°C (96-97.5°F)

C. 34.5-35.4°C (94-95.7°F)

Q3: Taking care of both the mother and the developing fetus is of utmost importance during pregnancy. We know that adequate nutrition plays a vital role in this journey. Among the listed nutrients, which one do we specifically consider as particularly crucial during pregnancy?

A. Calcium

B. Vitamin C

C. Folic acid

Q4: Obstetrical history plays an important role in assessing the risk factors and potential complications during pregnancy and childbirth. Which of the following obstetrical factors increases the likelihood of assisted delivery using forceps or vacuum?

A. Adolescent pregnancy

B. Multiparity

C. Postdates gestation

Q5: In providing culturally sensitive care during pregnancy, which of the following actions by the healthcare provider would be most appropriate?

A. Implementing standardized care without considering cultural differences

B. Recognizing and respecting the diverse beliefs and practices of different cultures

C. Encouraging the patient to conform to the healthcare provider's cultural norms

Q6: Which factor is considered a common cause of infertility in women?

A. Advanced maternal age

B. Multiparity

C. Postdates gestation

Q7: Which of the following is a physiologic change associated with pregnancy?

A. Increased blood volume

B. Decreased lung capacity

C. Reduced cardiac output

Q8: Which of the following is a known antepartum risk factor for complications during pregnancy?

A. Advanced maternal age

B. Primiparity

C. Male fetus

Q9: Which of the following methods is commonly used for fetal assessment during pregnancy?

A. Ultrasound

B. Urine analysis

C. Blood pressure measurement

Q10: Pregnancy is a transformative journey, and for some mothers-to-be with a history of obesity and bariatric surgery, there might be specific concerns. Let's explore the relationship between obesity, bariatric surgery, and pregnancy to identify the correct statement.

A) Obesity and bariatric surgery can lead to increased risks of gestational diabetes.

B) Pregnancy outcomes remain unaffected by obesity and bariatric surgery.

C) it's been observed that obesity and bariatric surgery may actually lower the chances of preterm birth.

D) Obesity and bariatric surgery are linked to decreased risks of cesarean delivery

Q11: Which of the following FHR patterns is considered abnormal and may indicate fetal distress?

A. Accelerations

B. Early decelerations

C. Late decelerations

Q12: Fetal heart rate abnormalities are important indicators of fetal well-being during labor. Which fetal heart rate pattern is characterized by a persistent fetal heart rate above 160 beats per minute?

A. Tachycardia

B. Bradycardia

C. Altered variability

Q13: During this transformative time, your body undergoes some incredible adjustments.

One fascinating process is known as involution, where your uterus gradually returns to its pre-pregnancy size by the end of the first week. Additionally, you might notice a vaginal discharge called lochia, which goes through color changes from lochia rubra to serosa and eventually to alba. These natural changes are your body's way of healing and preparing for the next stage.

A) The cervix, which dilated during birth, gradually closes over the next few weeks, allowing the body to recover.

B) After childbirth, something truly remarkable happens - the uterus starts a journey of involution, working its way back to its pre-pregnancy size by the end of the first week.

C) Breast engorgement may be a normal finding in the immediate postpartum period.

Q14: A postpartum woman presents with tachypnea and shortness of breath. Which physiologic change during the postpartum period could contribute to these symptoms?

A. Increased cardiac output

B. Decreased blood volume

C. Decreased respiratory rate

Q15: A postpartum woman is experiencing lightheadedness, dizziness, and a drop in blood pressure when changing positions from lying down to standing. Which physiological change during the postpartum period is likely contributing to these symptoms?

A. Increased red blood cell production

B. Decreased vascular resistance

C. Increased blood volume

Q16: A postpartum woman complains of frequent urination and a sense of urinary urgency. Which physiological change during the postpartum period is likely contributing to these symptoms?

A. Increased bladder capacity

B. Decreased bladder tone

C. Increased renal blood flow

Q17: A postpartum woman complains of constipation and abdominal discomfort following vaginal delivery. On assessment, her abdomen is soft and non-tender, and there are no signs of bowel obstruction. She reports passing small, hard stools infrequently. What is the most appropriate nursing intervention for this woman?

A. Encourage increased fluid intake and fiber-rich foods

B. Administer a stool softener as prescribed

C. Assist the woman with ambulation and gentle exercise

Q18: A postpartum woman reports severe perineal pain and discomfort following an episiotomy repair. On assessment, you note redness, swelling, and tenderness around the episiotomy site. What is the most likely cause of these symptoms?

A. Episiotomy infection

B. Hematoma formation

C. Episiotomy dehiscence

Q19: If the woman's hemoglobin is within normal limits during pregnancy, what is the recommended daily intake of elemental iron?

A. 30 mg of elemental iron

B. 60 mg of elemental iron

C. 120 mg of elemental iron

Q20: In the immediate postpartum period, what should a preeclamptic woman be closely monitored for?

A. Adult respiratory distress syndrome

B. Onset of seizures

C. Subdural hematoma

Q21: A postpartum woman who underwent a cesarean delivery is receiving postoperative care. Which nursing intervention is essential to include in her care plan?

A. Monitoring the incision site for signs of infection

B. Assisting with ambulation and promoting early mobilization

C. Providing education on breastfeeding techniques

Q22: A postpartum woman who had a prolonged labor and received epidural analgesia complains of severe headache that worsens when she sits up. Which condition should the nurse suspect?

A. Postpartum hemorrhage

B. Postpartum depression

C. Postural puncture headache

Q23: Which medication is commonly administered to manage diabetes in the postpartum period?

A. Insulin

B. Analgesics (Tylenol)

C. Antimicrobials

Q24: Which medication is commonly administered to prevent postpartum hemorrhage and promote uterine contractions?

A. Insulin

B. Analgesics (Tylenol)

C. Oxytocic

Q25: A postpartum woman who has undergone a cesarean section is experiencing moderate pain. Which medication is commonly administered as an analgesic in this situation?

A. Insulin

B. Analgesics (Tylenol)

C. Antimicrobials

Q26: Let's delve into the situation of a postpartum woman who's currently facing some medical considerations. After the joyous event of childbirth, she's dealing with both high blood pressure and edema, which can be concerning. Which potential drug interaction should the nurse be aware of when administering these medications?

A. Insulin

B. Analgesics (Tylenol)

C. Diuretics

Q27: A postpartum woman has been prescribed a diuretic medication to manage her fluid retention. The nurse is providing patient teaching about the medication. Which statement by the woman indicates an understanding of the teaching?

A. "I should take the diuretic medication with a meal to prevent stomach upset."

B. "I will monitor my blood pressure regularly while taking the diuretic medication."

C. "It is safe for me to consume foods high in potassium while on the diuretic medication."

Q28: As we delve into the world of maternal newborn nursing, let's explore the journey of a brave postpartum woman who's recently been diagnosed with gestational diabetes. It's a time of mixed emotions, as she navigates her new role as a mother while also managing this medical condition. The nurse is providing education about insulin administration. Which statement by the woman indicates a need for further teaching?

A. "I should rotate injection sites within the same anatomical area to prevent tissue damage."

B. "I will monitor my blood glucose levels regularly to adjust my insulin dosage if needed."

C. let's address a vital aspect of managing hypoglycemia.

Q29: A postpartum woman complains of pain, swelling, and discomfort in the perineal area. On assessment, the nurse notes perineal edema and pain. What is the appropriate nursing intervention for perineal edema and pain?

A. Applying ice packs to the perineal area

B. Encouraging frequent sits baths

C. Administer ring oral analgesics as prescribed

Q30: A postpartum woman reports experiencing painful bowel movements and constipation. Which nursing intervention is appropriate for managing constipation in the postpartum period?

A. Encouraging a high-fiber diet and increased fluid intake

B. Administering laxatives without prescription

C. Restricting the woman's physical activity

Q31: A postpartum woman reports experiencing severe perineal pain and discomfort. On assessment, the nurse observes swelling and redness in the perineal area. What complication should the nurse suspect based on these findings?

A. Bladder distention and urinary retention

B. Hemorrhoids

C. Perineal edema and pain

Q32: A postpartum woman is experiencing breast engorgement and discomfort. The nurse provides education on measures to relieve the symptoms. Which intervention should the nurse include in the teaching?

A. Apply warm compresses to the breasts before breastfeeding.

B. Limit breastfeeding time to 5 minutes on each breast.

C. Wash the breasts frequently with soap to keep them clean.

Q33: A postpartum woman asks the nurse about contraception options. The woman is exclusively breastfeeding her newborn and desires an effective and safe method of contraception. What method should the nurse recommend?

A. Combined hormonal contraceptives (birth control pills)

B. Intrauterine device (IUD)

C. Barrier methods (condoms)

Q34: A lactating mother expresses concern about the volume of breast milk she is producing. Which statement by the mother indicates a need for further education?

A. "I should breastfeed my baby on demand and not follow a strict feeding schedule."

B. "I can supplement with formula to ensure my baby is getting enough milk."

C. "I should avoid drinking plenty of fluids because it might decrease my milk supply."

Q35: A breastfeeding mother asks about the composition of breast milk. Which statement by the mother indicates a need for further education?

A. "Breast milk contains antibodies that help protect my baby against infections."

B. "The composition of breast milk changes over time to meet my baby's nutritional needs."

C. "Breast milk lacks essential nutrients, so I need to introduce solid foods early."

Q36: A new mother is learning about the normal breastfeeding process. Which step of the breastfeeding process involves the baby's ability to effectively extract milk from the breast?

A. Positioning

B. Latch On

C. Suck/Swallow Sequence

Q37: A lactation consultant is discussing the importance of a proper latch-on during breastfeeding. Which statement accurately describes the significance of a good latch-on?

A. "A proper latch-on ensures optimal milk transfer and helps prevent nipple soreness and damage."

B. "The latch-on technique has no impact on milk transfer as long as the baby is breastfeeding frequently."

C. "Latch-on primarily affects the mother's comfort during breastfeeding and has minimal impact on milk supply."

Q38: A lactating mother is experiencing difficulty with hand expression of breast milk. The nurse suspects that incorrect positioning may be the underlying issue. Which statement accurately describes the importance of proper positioning in hand expression?

A. "Proper positioning ensures a comfortable and relaxed hand posture, which promotes effective milk flow and prevents hand fatigue."

B. "Positioning plays a minimal role in hand expression; the technique itself is more critical for successful milk removal."

C. "Positioning primarily affects the infant's latch during breastfeeding and has minimal impact on hand expression."

Q39: Linda, a postpartum woman, seeks guidance on breast care to ensure optimal breastfeeding. The nurse explains the key points of breast care to promote lactation and prevent complications. Which key point is essential for Linda to understand regarding expressing and storing breast milk?

A. Use of Supplementary Feedings

B. Use of Breastfeeding Devices

C. Expressing and Storing Breast Milk

Q40: Emily, a new mother, expresses concern about her ability to breastfeed due to her inverted nipples. She seeks advice on using breastfeeding devices to facilitate breastfeeding. The nurse explains the key points of breastfeeding devices to address Emily's concerns. Which key point should the nurse emphasize when discussing the use of breastfeeding devices?

A. Use of Supplementary Feedings

B. Use of Breastfeeding Devices

C. Expressing and Storing Breast Milk

Q41: A breastfeeding mother is experiencing nipple pain and discomfort during feeding. Which key point of nipple care should be recommended to alleviate the symptoms and promote optimal breastfeeding?

A. Use of Complementary Feedings

B. Use of Breastfeeding Devices

C. Ensure that the infant has proper latch on to the breast

Q42: A breastfeeding mother has been diagnosed with a severe bacterial infection requiring immediate treatment with antibiotics Where we must navigate the complexities of breastfeeding and its potential challenges for the mother and her newborn.

A. Maternal complications

B. Latch-on problems

C. Therapeutic medications

Q43: A newborn infant's mother has a history of perinatal substance abuse and is currently undergoing treatment. Where we must navigate the complexities of breastfeeding and its potential challenges for the mother and her newborn.

A. Insufficient milk supply

B. Breast engorgement

C. Perinatal substance abuse

Q44: let's immerse ourselves in a poignant scene that captures the essence of this extraordinary journey. Picture this: a tiny, delicate newborn, a beacon of hope and promise, has found their way into the neonatal intensive care unit (NICU) where expert care and vigilant monitoring await. The emotions are running high for both the baby and the mother as they embark on this unexpected journey together. This practice helps to promote: This practice helps to promote:

A. Maternal-infant bonding

B. Maternal sleep deprivation

C. Maternal complications

Q45: A term newborn presents with yellowing of the skin and sclera. The healthcare provider suspects hyperbilirubinemia. Which intervention is appropriate for managing hyperbilirubinemia in the newborn?

A. Encourage frequent breastfeeding

B. Administer intravenous antibiotics

C. Initiate phototherapy

Q46: A newborn is experiencing jitteriness, poor feeding, and lethargy shortly after birth. The nurse suspects hypoglycemia. What is the recommended initial intervention for managing hypoglycemia in the newborn?

A. Administer a bolus of formula

B. Provide glucose gel orally

C. Place the newborn in a radiant warmer

Q47: Which of the following is a normal characteristic of parents during the postpartum period?

A. Feeling overwhelmed and uncertain about their parenting abilities

B. Experiencing mood swings and tearfulness

C. Demonstrating increased self-confidence and competence

Q48: During postpartum assessment, a nurse observes a woman who recently gave birth. The nurse notices that the woman's breasts are engorged, firm, and warm to the touch. The nurse recognizes this as a normal finding in the immediate postpartum period due to increased blood and lymph flow to the breasts. The nurse's priority action should be to:

A. Encourage the woman to breastfeed frequently to promote milk letdown and relieve discomfort.

B. Apply cold packs to the breasts to reduce swelling and discomfort.

C. Administer pain medication to alleviate the discomfort associated with breast engorgement.

Q49: During postpartum assessment, a nurse is providing education to a woman who recently gave birth regarding maternal role transition. The nurse explains the concept of the "taking hold" phase, which typically occurs within the first few weeks after childbirth. The nurse asks the woman to identify the characteristics associated with this phase. Which response by the woman indicates an understanding of the "taking hold" phase?

A. "During this phase, I may feel overwhelmed and anxious about my ability to care for my newborn."

B. "I will experience a strong emotional bond with my baby and have a deep sense of satisfaction."

Cathi's phase is characterized by increased confidence in my role as a mother and actively seeking information about baby care."

Q50: A postpartum nurse is providing education to a family with a newborn and an older sibling. The nurse discusses the sibling's response to the new baby and provides guidance on fostering a positive sibling relationship. Which statement by the parents indicates an understanding of promoting positive sibling response?

A. "We should encourage our older child to participate in baby care activities, such as diaper changes and bottle feeding."

B. "It's best to keep the older child away from the newborn to prevent potential jealousy and rivalry."

C. "We should tell our older child that the new baby will replace them as the center of our attention."

51: A postpartum nurse is providing education to a woman about barriers and alterations to parent/infant interactions. The nurse explains that maternal factors can impact the quality of parent/infant interactions. Which statement by the nurse accurately describes a potential barrier to parent/infant interactions?

A. "Maternal exhaustion and sleep deprivation can hinder the mother's ability to engage with her newborn."

B. "Feeling a strong emotional bond with the baby is not necessary for effective parent/infant interactions."

C. "It is best for the mother to limit physical contact with the baby to prevent dependency."

Q52: A postpartum nurse is providing education on life-style factors affecting family integration. The nurse discusses the impact of substance abuse on family dynamics and integration. Which statement accurately describes the effect of substance abuse on family integration?

A. "Substance abuse can enhance communication and bonding among family members."

B. "Substance abuse often leads to improved financial stability within the family."

C. "Substance abuse can disrupt family relationships and hinder healthy integration."

Q53: A postpartum nurse is discussing cultural factors affecting family integration with a group of expectant parents from diverse backgrounds. The nurse explains that cultural practices can significantly impact family dynamics and integration. Which statement accurately describes a cultural factor that can influence family integration?

A. "In some cultures, extended family members play a minimal role in supporting the new parents."

B. "Cultural norms often prioritize individual autonomy over collective decision-making."

C. "Cultural practices universally promote identical roles and responsibilities for all family members."

Q54: A postpartum nurse is providing education on intimate partner violence to a group of new mothers. Which statement accurately describes the characteristics of intimate partner violence?

A. "Intimate partner violence is limited to physical abuse and does not involve emotional or psychological harm."

B. ""Intimate partner violence is a deeply concerning issue that encompasses not only physical abuse but also extends to emotional, sexual, and financial abuse.

C. "Intimate partner violence is primarily experienced by men and rarely affects women."

Q55: A mother who is experiencing postpartum depression is struggling to bond with her newborn. Which psychosocial intervention would be most appropriate to enhance family dynamics in this situation?

A "Encourage the mother to embrace precious skin-to-skin contact with her baby for a strong bonding experience.

B. Advising the mother to limit her interactions with the baby to avoid overwhelming feelings of sadness.

C. Suggesting that the mother seek individual therapy to address her emotional challenges separately from the baby.

Q56: A couple has made the decision to place their newborn for adoption. Which ethical principle should the healthcare provider prioritize when supporting the couple during this process?

A. Autonomy

B. Beneficence

C. Nonmaleficence

Q57: A nurse is providing care for a woman who has experienced a stillbirth. Which intervention is most appropriate to support the mother's grieving process?

A. Encouraging the mother to avoid talking about her feelings to prevent further emotional distress.

B. Providing resources and information about support groups or counseling services specializing in perinatal grief.

C. Discouraging the mother from spending time with her baby after birth to minimize emotional attachment.

Q58: Q55: A compassionate nurse finds herself caring for a postpartum woman who is facing a deeply concerning and potentially life-threatening situation – severe postpartum hemorrhage. The physician recommends a blood transfusion to stabilize her condition. Which ethical principle is most relevant in this situation?

A. Autonomy

B. Beneficence

C. Nonmaleficence

Q59: A newborn is born with a heart rate of 90 beats per minute, irregular respirations, weak muscle tone, and cyanosis. Which condition does this newborn most likely present with?

A. Transient tachypnea of the newborn

B. Meconium aspiration syndrome

C. Transition delay

Q60: A nurse is performing a newborn assessment and notices that the baby has a single transverse palmar crease and epicanthal folds. What condition should the nurse suspect?

A. Down syndrome (Trisomy 21)

B. Cleft palate

C. Neural tube defect

Q61: A nurse is caring for a newborn in the delivery room. Which action would be most effective in promoting thermoregulation in the newborn?

A. Placing the newborn under a radiant warmer immediately after birth.

B. Delaying skin-to-skin contact until the newborn's temperature stabilizes.

C. Administering warm intravenous fluids to the newborn.

Q62: A newborn is being evaluated for possible sepsis. Which laboratory finding is indicative of an infection in a newborn?

A. Elevated white blood cell (WBC) count

B. Decreased bilirubin levels

C. Increased glucose levels

Q63: A newborn is diagnosed with hypoglycemia. Which laboratory value would confirm this diagnosis?

A. Blood glucose level of 80 mg/dL

B. Blood glucose level of 60 mg/dL

C. Blood glucose level of 120 mg/dL

Correct answer: B. Blood glucose level of 60 mg/dL

Q64: A nurse is assessing a newborn and performing a gestational age assessment. Which assessment finding is most indicative of a preterm newborn?

A. Lanugo covering the body

B. Flexed posture of the extremities

C. Fused eyelids

Q65: A newborn is being evaluated for gestational age using the New Ballard Score. Which assessment finding would indicate a post-term newborn?

A. Abundant vernix caseosa

B. Creases over the sole of the foot

C. Recoiled ears

Q66: A nurse is conducting a neurobehavioral assessment on a newborn. Which behavior would indicate a normal response to stimuli?

A. Crying in response to a loud noise

B. Consolable and alert when touched

C. Lack of response to light stimulation

Q67: During a sensory assessment, a newborn exhibits a strong rooting reflex. What is the purpose of this reflex?

A. To protect the airway during feeding

B. To facilitate visual tracking of objects

C. To stimulate the startle response

Q68: Removing a neonate from an incubator for procedures without the use of an overhead warmer will result in heat loss by:

A. Convection

B. Evaporation

C. Radiation

Q69: When providing cord care for a newborn, which intervention should the nurse recommend?

A. Cleanse the cord stump with alcohol after every diaper change.

B. Keep the cord stump dry and exposed to air.

C. Apply antibiotic ointment to the cord stump daily.

Q70: A newborn is experiencing difficulty passing stools. The nurse suspects the newborn may have meconium ileus, a common variation in newborn elimination. Which condition is associated with meconium ileus?

A. Constipation

B. Hirschsprung's disease

C. Gastroesophageal reflux

Q71: A parent asks the nurse about the benefits of circumcision for their newborn son. Which information should the nurse provide?

A. "Circumcision can reduce urinary tract infection risk in newborns."

B. "Circumcision eliminates the need for proper hygiene care of the penis."

C. "Circumcision improves breastfeeding success rates."

Q72: A newborn is experiencing excessive crying and restlessness. Which comfort measure should the nurse implement to provide relief?

A. Swaddling the newborn snugly in a blanket

B. Administering a pacifier to the newborn

C. Applying a cool washcloth to the newborn's forehead

Q73: A parent asks the nurse about soothing techniques for a fussy newborn. Which recommendation should the nurse provide?

A. Use gentle rocking or swaying motions to calm the newborn.

B. Provide loud and stimulating toys to distract the newborn.

C. Keep the environment quiet and dimly lit to promote relaxation.

Q74: A newborn is being screened for congenital heart defects (CHD). Which screening method is commonly used to assess CHD in newborns?

A. Electrocardiogram (ECG)

B. Echocardiogram (echo)

C. Chest X-ray

Q75: A parent asks the nurse about the appropriate car seat for their newborn. What is the nurse's best response?

A. "A rear-facing car seat is safest for newborns up to 2 years old or until they reach the car seat's weight and height limits."

B. "A forward-facing car seat with a harness is suitable for newborns as long as they are securely fastened."

C. "Using a booster seat without a backrest is the safest option for newborns."

Q76: A newborn is at risk for developing skin breakdown due to prolonged contact with moisture. Which intervention should the nurse prioritize to prevent skin breakdown?

A. Applying a moisture barrier cream to the newborn's skin

B. Frequent diaper changes to keep the skin dry

C. Massaging the newborn's skin with lotion after each bath

Q77: A parent asks the nurse about the best way to care for their newborn's umbilical cord stump. What is the nurse's best response?

A. "To ensure your little one's umbilical cord stump stays healthy, simply use a clean, dry cloth to gently wipe it and keep it clean and dry."

B. "Applying antibiotic ointment to the umbilical cord stump is recommended to prevent infection."

C. "To safeguard the umbilical cord stump from contamination, covering it with a bandage is advisable."

Q78: A nurse is providing education to parents about safe sleep practices for their newborn. Which statement by the parents indicates understanding of safe sleep?

A. "We will place our newborn to sleep on their back in a separate crib or bassinet."

B. "We will use soft bedding and pillows to make our newborn more comfortable during sleep."

C. "We will allow our newborn to sleep in the same bed with us to promote bonding."

Q79: A parent asks the nurse about tummy time for their newborn. What is the nurse's best response?

A. "Tummy time is important for strengthening your newborn's neck and upper body muscles."

B. "It is best to avoid tummy time until your newborn can roll over independently."

C. "Tummy time should be done immediately after feeding to aid in digestion."

Q80: A nurse is preparing to administer oral sucrose to a newborn for a painful procedure. What is the primary purpose of administering oral sucrose?

A. To provide analgesia and reduce pain response in the newborn

B. To promote digestion and improve feeding tolerance in the newborn

C. To enhance immune function and prevent infections in the newborn

Q81: A newborn is receiving vitamin K as a routine prophylactic medication. What is the purpose of administering vitamin K to a newborn?

A. To prevent bleeding disorders and promote blood clotting

B. To support bone development and prevent rickets

C. To enhance the immune response and prevent infections

Q82: A newborn is delivered and appears pale, floppy, and is not breathing. What is the appropriate initial action by the healthcare provider?

A. Administer positive-pressure ventilation

B. Administer chest compressions

C. Provide tactile stimulation

Q83: A newborn is born with meconium-stained amniotic fluid. What is the next step in the management of this newborn?

A. Administer oxygen via a face mask

B. Perform endotracheal intubation and suction the airway

C. Initiate cardiopulmonary resuscitation (CPR)

Q4: During the resuscitation of a newborn, which step takes priority to ensure a patent airway?

A. Administering positive-pressure ventilation

B. Placing the newborn in the sniffing position

C. Performing endotracheal intubation

Q85: In the management of resuscitation, what is the next step after establishing a patent airway?

A. Administering chest compressions

B. Assessing the heart rate

C. Initiating positive-pressure ventilation

Q86: Which medication is commonly administered to newborns as prophylaxis for vitamin K deficiency bleeding?

A. Oral sucrose

B. Vitamin K

C. Hepatitis B vaccine

Q87: In the management of respiratory distress syndrome (RDS) in newborns, which medication is frequently used to improve lung function?

A. Ibuprofen

B. Surfactant

C. Epinephrine

Q88: After providing respiratory support to a newborn, which assessment finding indicates an effective intervention?

A. Decreased heart rate

B. Cyanosis of the lips

C. Increased respiratory effort

Q89: A newborn received phototherapy for hyperbilirubinemia. What finding indicates the effectiveness of the intervention?

A. Persistent jaundice

B. Decreased bilirubin levels

C. Increased lethargy

Q90: The Apgar score is a quick assessment of a newborn's overall well-being at what time after birth?

A. 5 minutes

B. 10 minutes

C. 15 minutes

Q91: The Apgar score evaluates which of the following criteria in a newborn?

A. Heart rate, respiratory effort, muscle tone, reflex irritability, and color

B. The Apgar score evaluates heart rate, respiratory rate, blood pressure, temperature, and weight.

C. Heart rate, temperature, muscle tone, gestational age, and feeding ability

Q92: Postpartum hemorrhage is defined as a blood loss of how much or more within the first 24 hours after childbirth?

A. 500 ml

B. 1000 ml

C. 1500 ml

Q93: The most common cause of postpartum hemorrhage is:

A. Uterine atony

B. Placenta accrete

C. Coagulation disorders

Q94: Thrombophlebitis is a condition characterized by inflammation and blood clot formation in which of the following blood vessels?

A. Arteries

B. Veins

C. Capillaries

Q95: The most common site for thrombophlebitis in the postpartum period is the:

A. Lower extremities

B. Upper extremities

C. Pelvic region

Q96: As a caring and attentive nurse, you understand the significance of postpartum care for new mothers. Among the options below, which factor is considered the primary risk factor for postpartum thrombophlebitis?

A. Cesarean birth

B. Maternal age over 35

C. Prolonged labor

Q97: Pulmonary embolus is a potentially life-threatening condition characterized by:

A. Inflammation of the lungs

B. Formation of blood clots in the pulmonary arteries

C. Infection of the lung tissue

Q98: The most common source of blood clots that lead to pulmonary embolus is:

A. Deep vein thrombosis in the legs

B. Coronary artery disease

C. Atrial fibrillation

Q99: Disseminated intravascular coagulation (DIC) is a condition characterized by:

A. Abnormal bleeding and clotting throughout the body

B. Blood vessel inflammation.

C. Elevated white blood cell count

Q100: DIC can be triggered by various maternal conditions, including:

A. Preterm labor

B. Gestational diabetes

C. Urinary tract infection

Q101: HELLP syndrome is a severe complication of pregnancy characterized by:

A. Hemolysis, Elevated Liver enzymes, Low Platelet count

B. Hyperemesis, Elevated Lipids, Low Protein levels

C. Hypertension, Elevated Leukocytes, Low Progesterone levels

Q102: HELLP syndrome most commonly occurs in:

A. First-time mothers

B. Women with a history of chronic hypertension

C. Women with gestational diabetes

Q103: A hematoma is a localized collection of blood outside blood vessels, often caused by:

A. Constriction of blood vessels

B. Excessive bleeding during delivery

C. Inadequate oxygen supply to tissues

Q104: The most common site for a perineal hematoma is:

A. Vagina

B. Uterus

C. Perineum

Q105: The signs and symptoms of a perineal hematoma may include:

A. Severe pain and swelling

B. Vaginal bleeding

C. Elevated blood pressure

Q106: Chronic hypertension is defined as high blood pressure that is diagnosed:

A. Before pregnancy or before 20 weeks' gestation

B. During the first trimester of pregnancy

C. After 28 weeks' gestation

Q107: Women with chronic hypertension have an increased risk of developing:

A. Gestational diabetes

B. Preterm labor

C. Placental abruption

Q108: Chronic hypertension during pregnancy is associated with an increased risk of:

A. Fetal growth restriction

B. Macrosomia (large-for-gestational-age baby)

C. Postpartum hemorrhage

Q109: Gestational hypertension is defined as the onset of hypertension after:

A. 12 weeks of gestation

B. 20 weeks of gestation

C. 28 weeks of gestation

Q110: Women with gestational hypertension are at increased risk of developing:

A. Preterm birth

B. Postpartum hemorrhage

C. Gestational diabetes

Q111: Eclampsia is defined as the onset of seizures in a woman with:

A. Gestational hypertension

B. Chronic hypertension

C. Preeclampsia

Q112: Eclampsia is characterized by the presence of:

A. Proteinuria

B. Hypotension

C. Hyperglycemia

Q113: Endometritis is defined as an infection of the:

A. Uterine lining

B. Fallopian tubes

C. Ovaries

Q114: The most common causative organism of postpartum endometritis is:

A. Group B Streptococcus

B. Escherichia coli

C. Staphylococcus aureus

Q115: Wound infection in the postpartum period most commonly occurs in the:

A. Episiotomy site

B. Abdominal incision

C. Breastfeeding nipples

Q116: Risk factors for developing a wound infection include:

A. Obesity

B. Primiparity

C. Maternal age under 20

Q117: Clinical manifestations of a wound infection may include:

A. Increased redness and warmth around the incision

B. Purulent drainage from the incision

C. Worsening pain at the incision site

Q118: Septic pelvic thrombophlebitis is an infection and inflammation of the veins in the pelvis. It most commonly occurs in the:

A. Uterine veins

B. Ovarian veins

C. Vaginal veins

Q119: Risk factors for developing septic pelvic thrombophlebitis include:

A. Cesarean section delivery

B. Maternal age over 35

C. Primigravity

Q120: Clinical manifestations of septic pelvic thrombophlebitis may include:

A. Pelvic pain and tenderness

B. Fever and chills

C. Palpitations and dizziness

Q121: Urinary tract infections (UTIs) are commonly seen in the postpartum period. The most common causative organism for postpartum UTIs is:

A. Escherichia coli

B. Staphylococcus aureus

C. Streptococcus pyogenes

Q122: Risk factors for developing a postpartum UTI include:

A. Prolonged labor

B. History of UTIs

C. Primiparity

Q123: Clinical manifestations of a postpartum UTI may include:

A. Dysuria (painful urination)

B. Lower abdominal pain

C. Urinary frequency

Q124: Women with gestational diabetes are at an increased risk of developing which of the following complications during pregnancy?

A. Preterm labor

B. Macrosomia (large birth weight)

C. Placenta previa

Q125: Gestational diabetes is characterized by:

A. Elevated blood glucose levels during pregnancy

B. Preexisting diabetes prior to pregnancy

C. Low blood glucose levels during pregnancy

Q126: Postpartum sleep disturbances can be caused by various factors. What could be a frequent cause of sleep disturbances in postpartum women?

A. Hormonal changes

B. Lack of exercise

C. Excessive caffeine intake

Q127: Sleep deprivation in the postpartum period can contribute to the development of:

A. Postpartum depression

B. Gestational diabetes

C. Preterm labor

Q128: Which sleep position is recommended for breastfeeding mothers to optimize comfort and safety?

A. Supine position

B. Prone position

C. Side-lying position

Q129: Postpartum depression is a mood disorder that typically occurs within the first year after childbirth. What is a prevalent symptom often experienced in postpartum depression?

A. Excessive happiness and euphoria

B. Loss of interest in activities

C. Difficulty Alling asleep but feeling refreshed upon waking

Q130: Postpartum psychosis is a rare but severe psychiatric disorder that occurs shortly after childbirth. Which of the following is a characteristic symptom of postpartum psychosis?

A. Mild mood swings

B. Delusions or hallucinations

C. Fatigue and lack of energy

Q131: Postpartum depression can have significant implications for maternal-infant bonding and infant development Untreated postpartum depression can have significant implications, potentially leading to which of the following outcome?

A. Improved cognitive development in the infant

B. Enhanced maternal self-esteem and confidence

C. Impaired mother-infant attachment

Q132: Substance abuse during pregnancy can have far-reaching consequences for both the mother and the developing fetus. Among the following substances, which one is linked to an elevated risk of preterm birth and low birth weight?

A. Alcohol

B. Marijuana

C. Tobacco

Q133: A pregnant woman who uses illicit substances is at risk for developing a substance use disorder. Which of the following is a characteristic feature of substance use disorder?

A. Controlled and occasional use of the substance

B. Tolerance and withdrawal symptoms

C. Moderate use without any negative consequences

Q134: Cyanotic heart disease refers to a group of congenital heart defects that result in decreased oxygenation of blood and cyanosis. Which of the following is a characteristic sign of cyanotic heart disease in a newborn?

A. Bluish discoloration of the skin and lips

B. Excessive sweating during feeding

C. Rapid weight gain

Q135: Cyanotic heart disease is a group of congenital heart defects characterized by reduced oxygenation of blood. Which of the following is an example of cyanotic heart disease?

A. Ventricular septal defect (VSD)

B. Atrial septal defect (ASD)

C. Transposition of the great arteries (TGA)

Q136: Cyanotic heart disease can lead to various complications in newborns. Which of the following is a potential complication associated with cyanotic heart disease?

A. Hypoglycemia

B. Respiratory distress syndrome

C. Gastrointestinal obstruction

Q137: A newborn is diagnosed with ventricular septal defect (VSD), an a cyanotic heart disease. Which of the following accurately describes VSD?

A. An abnormal connection between the aorta and pulmonary artery.

B. An abnormal opening between the ventricles.

C. Narrowing of the pulmonary valve.

Q138: Apnea is a common respiratory complication in newborns that can lead to life-threatening situations. Which of the following statements accurately describes apnea in newborns?

A. Apnea is a prolonged cessation of breathing that lasts for more than 20 seconds.

B. Apnea is a brief pause in breathing that lasts for less than 10 seconds.

C. Apnea is characterized by shallow breathing with an increased respiratory rate.

Q139: Transient Tachypnea of the Newborn (TTN) is a respiratory complication commonly observed in newborns. Which of the following accurately describes TTN?

A. TTN is a condition characterized by persistent tachycardia in newborns.

B. TTN is a transient elevation in blood pressure during the first few hours after birth.

C. TTN is a self-limiting respiratory disorder caused by delayed clearance of fetal lung fluid.

Q140: Pneumothorax, a potential respiratory complication in newborns, can be a concerning condition for their well-being. Can you identify the accurate description of pneumothorax?

A. Is pneumothorax best described as a condition characterized by an infection of the lung tissue, posing risks to the newborn's respiratory health?

B. Is pneumothorax best described as the accumulation of air in the pleural space, leading to lung collapse and potentially causing respiratory distress in the newborn?

C. Is pneumothorax best described as the narrowing or constriction of the bronchial tubes, potentially resulting in breathing difficulties for the newborn?

Q141: Meconium Aspiration Syndrome (MAS) is a respiratory complication that can occur in newborns. Which of the following accurately describes meconium aspiration?

A. Meconium aspiration is the inhalation of amniotic fluid during delivery.

B. Meconium aspiration is the presence of excessive mucus in the newborn's airways.

C. Meconium aspiration is the aspiration of meconium into the lungs before or during birth.

Q142: Seizures in newborns can be a sign of neurological dysfunction. Which of the following accurately describes seizures in newborns?

A. Seizures in newborns are typically caused by gastrointestinal issues.

B. Seizures in newborns commonly occur and typically do not require medical attention.

C. Seizures in newborns can indicate an underlying neurological condition or brain injury.

Q143: Jitteriness in a newborn can be a concerning sign. Which of the following accurately describes jitteriness in newborns?

A. Jitteriness is a normal behavior and does not require any intervention.

B. Jitteriness is a sign of gastrointestinal discomfort in newborns.

C. Jitteriness can be a manifestation of neurological issues or metabolic disturbances in newborns.

Q144: Intracranial hemorrhage in a newborn can be a serious complication. Which of the following accurately describes intracranial hemorrhage in newborns?

A. Intracranial hemorrhage is a normal finding in the immediate postpartum period.

B. Intracranial hemorrhage can occur due to trauma during delivery or underlying medical conditions.

C. Intracranial hemorrhage is a benign condition that does not require any intervention.

Q145: As a nurse caring for expectant parents, you learn about neural tube defects (NTDs), a group of congenital abnormalities that affect the development of the fetal neural tube. Now, your task is to identify which statement accurately describes neural tube defects:

A. Are neural tube defects primarily caused by genetic factors and have no association with maternal factors?

B. Can neural tube defects occur due to both genetic and environmental factors, including folic acid deficiency?

C. Are neural tube defects rare occurrences with no known risk factors?

Q146: A nurse is caring for a newborn who has been exposed to illicit substances during pregnancy. Which of the following signs or symptoms would the nurse expect to assess in a substance-abused neonate?

A. Lethargy and decreased muscle tone

B. Excessive crying and irritability

C. Normal feeding and weight gain

Q147: A nurse is assessing a newborn and suspects the presence of an intestinal obstruction. Which of the following clinical manifestations would the nurse expect to observe in this newborn?

A. Projectile vomiting and abdominal distension

B. Excessive weight gain and constipation

C. Decreased appetite and loose stools

Q148: A newborn is diagnosed with Hirschsprung's disease. Which of the following statements accurately describes this condition?

A Hirschsprung's disease is a condition present since birth, characterized by the absence of nerve cells in the rectum and lower colon.

B. It is a condition where the intestines twist upon themselves, causing obstruction and compromised blood supply.

C In this condition, the abdominal wall fails to close properly, leading to the protrusion of abdominal contents.

Q149: A newborn is diagnosed with iron-deficiency anemia. Which of the following interventions should the nurse include in the care plan?

A. Administering iron supplements and promoting iron-rich foods

B. Encouraging increased fluid intake and providing electrolyte solutions

C. Implementing strict infection control measures and administering antibiotics

Q150: A newborn is diagnosed with vitamin K deficiency. Which intervention should the nurse prioritize in the care of this newborn?

A. Administering vitamin K supplementation

B. Monitoring blood glucose levels

C. Initiating phototherapy

"Q151: A newborn is at risk for vitamin K deficiency due to maternal use of anticonvulsant medication during pregnancy. Which action should the nurse take to prevent vitamin K deficiency In this newborn?"

A. Administering an intramuscular injection of vitamin K at birth

B. Providing oral vitamin K drops daily for the first week of life

C. Encouraging increased intake of vitamin K-rich foods

Q152: A newborn is diagnosed with hyperbilirubinemia. Which intervention should the nurse prioritize in the care of this newborn?

A. Initiating phototherapy

B. Administering intravenous antibiotics

C. Performing a lumbar puncture

Q153: A newborn is diagnosed with ABO incompatibility. Which blood group combination is most commonly associated with this condition?

A. Mother: O positive, Father: A positive

B. Mother: A positive, Father: AB negative

C. Mother: B negative, Father: O positive

Q154: Which antibody is involved in ABO incompatibility reactions in newborns?

A. Anti-A antibody

B. Anti-B antibody

C. Anti-Rh antibody

Q155: Hemolytic disease of the newborn is most commonly caused by which of the following?

A. ABO incompatibility

B. Rh incompatibility

C. Maternal rubella infection

Q156: Which enzyme deficiency is associated with glucose-6-phosphate dehydrogenase (G6PD) deficiency?

A. Glucose-6-phosphatase

B. Glucose-6-phosphate isomerase

C G6PD deficiency results from a lack of the glucose-6-phosphate dehydrogenase enzyme.

Q157: Which population is at a higher risk of G6PD deficiency?

A. Females

B. Males

C. Premature infants

Q158: Which of the following is a characteristic feature of polycythemia in a newborn?

A. Elevated hematocrit level

B. Low platelet count

C. Decreased red blood cell size

Q159: A nurse is caring for a neonate with polycythemia. Which clinical manifestation should the nurse monitor for as a potential complication?

A. Hypotension

B. Hypoglycemia

C Hypoxemia

Q160: A newborn is diagnosed with hyper viscosity "What key characteristic feature is associated with hyper viscosity in a newborn?"

A. Elevated red blood cell count

B. Decreased platelet count

C. Increased white blood cell size

"Q161: As a nurse caring for a newborn, you receive a diagnosis of thrombocytopenia for the baby. Can you identify which of the following features is a characteristic of this condition?"

A. Elevated platelet count

B. Decreased platelet count

C. Increased red blood cell size

Q162: A newborn is suspected to have neonatal sepsis. Which of the following is the most common route of transmission for neonatal sepsis?

A. Vertical transmission from the mother during childbirth

B. Ingestion of contaminated breast milk

C. Airborne transmission from healthcare providers

Q163: A newborn is suspected to have an infectious disease. Which laboratory test is commonly used to evaluate the presence of infection and monitor the response to treatment in newborns?

A. Neonatal complete blood count (CBC)

B. Neonatal blood glucose level

C. Neonatal liver function test

Q164: A nurse is reviewing the results of a neonatal complete blood count (CBC) and differential. Which component of the CBC provides information about the presence of infection?

A. White blood cell (WBC) count

B. Red blood cell (RBC) count

C. Hemoglobin level

Q165: A newborn is suspected to have meningitis. "Which diagnostic procedure is frequently employed to collect cerebrospinal fluid (CSF) for analysis in a newborn suspected to have meningitis?"

A. Lumbar puncture

B. Blood culture

C. Urine analysis

Q166: A nurse is preparing a newborn for a lumbar puncture. What position should the nurse place the newborn in for the procedure?

A. Lateral recumbent position

B. Supine position with flexed knees

C. Prone position with extended legs

Q167: A newborn is diagnosed with congenital cytomegalovirus infection. Which of the following is a common manifestation of CMV infection in a newborn?

A. Enlarged liver and spleen

B. Microcephaly and developmental delay

C. Cough and respiratory distress

Q168: A newborn is diagnosed with congenital syphilis. What signs or symptoms are commonly linked to this condition?

A. Jaundice and hepatomegaly

B. Microcephaly and neurologic abnormalities

C. Respiratory distress and pneumonia

Q169: A pregnant woman with human papillomavirus (HPV) infection asks if the infection can be transmitted to her newborn during birth. What is the appropriate response by the healthcare provider?

A. "HPV is not typically transmitted to the newborn during birth."

B. "The risk of HPV transmission can be reduced by performing a cesarean section."

C. "There is no need to worry about HPV transmission as it is a harmless infection."

Q170: A newborn is diagnosed with a bacterial infection and is prescribed an antibiotic. What adverse effect is common with antibiotic therapy in newborns?

A. Bradycardia

B. Hyperglycemia

C. Hypothermia

Q171: A pregnant woman is diagnosed with group B streptococcus (GBS) colonization. What intervention is recommended to prevent GBS infection in the newborn?

A. Administration of prophylactic antibiotics during labor

B. Delaying the initiation of breastfeeding until GBS is cleared

C. Isolating the newborn in a separate room to prevent transmission

Q172: A newborn is experiencing symptoms of jitteriness, poor feeding, and lethargy shortly after birth. These signs are indicative of:

A. Hypoglycemia

B. Hyperglycemia

C. Hyperbilirubinemia

Q173: Which of the following conditions is characterized by a genetic defect in the metabolism of certain substances, leading to the accumulation of toxic byproducts?

A. Phenylketonuria (PKU)

B. Down syndrome

C. Cystic fibrosis

Q174 "As a couple seeks genetic counseling due to their family history of a genetic condition, the genetic counselor explains that if the condition follows an autosomal recessive inheritance pattern, what is the likelihood that their child will be affected if both parents are carriers?

A. 25%

B. 50%

C. 75%

Q175: An infant is born to a mother with poorly controlled diabetes. Which of the following conditions is commonly seen in infants of diabetic mothers?

A. Hypoglycemia

B. Hyperglycemia

C. Hypocalcemia

Test 1 Answer Key

1	A	27	B	53	A
2	A	28	C	54	B
3	C	29	B	55	A
4	C	30	A	56	A
5	B	31	C	57	B
6	A	32	A	58	B
7	A	33	B	59	C
8	A	34	C	60	A
9	A	35	C	61	A
10	A	36	C	62	A
11	C	37	A	63	C
12	A	38	A	64	C
13	B	39	C	65	B
14	B	40	B	66	B
15	B	41	C	67	A
16	B	42	C	68	C
17	A	43	C	69	B
18	B	44	A	70	B
19	B	45	C	71	A
20	B	46	B	72	A
21	A	47	C	73	A
22	C	48	A	74	B
23	A	49	C	75	A
24	C	50	A	76	B
25	B	51	A	77	A
26	C	52	C	78	A

79	A	106	A	133	B
80	A	107	C	134	A
81	A	108	A	135	C
82	C	109	B	136	B
83	B	110	A	137	B
84	B	111	C	138	A
85	C	112	A	139	C
86	B	113	A	140	B
87	B	114	B	141	C
88	A	115	B	142	C
89	B	116	A	143	C
90	A	117	B	144	B
91	A	118	B	145	B
92	B	119	A	146	B
93	A	120	A	147	A
94	B	121	A	148	A
95	A	122	B	149	A
96	A	123	A	150	A
97	B	124	B	151	A
98	A	125	A	152	A
99	A	126	A	153	A
100	A	127	A	154	B
101	A	128	C	155	B
102	B	129	B	156	C
103	B	130	B	157	B
104	C	131	C	158	A
105	A	132	C	159	C

160	A		**166**	B		**172**	A
161	B		**167**	B		**173**	A
162	A		**168**	B		**174**	B
163	A		**169**	A		**175**	A
164	A		**170**	B			
165	A		**171**	A			

Maternal Newborn Nursing Exam Practice Test 2

Q1: During pregnancy which factors are associated with an increased likelihood of preterm birth and low birth weight in newborns?

A. Advanced maternal age

B. Nulliparity

C. History of preterm birth

Q2: During pregnancy, a woman's basal metabolic rate (BMR) should:

A. Decrease

B. Increase

C. Remain stable

3: As a nurse, taking care of pregnant individuals you are well aware of the significance of ensuring adequate nutrition to support the health and development of both the mother and the baby. Can you identify the essential nutrient crucial for forming red blood cells and preventing iron-deficiency anemia during pregnancy?

A. Calcium

B. Vitamin C

C. Iron

Q4: Obstetrical history is an important aspect of assessing a woman's pregnancy and birth risk factors. Which of the following factors is associated with an increased risk of postpartum hemorrhage?

A. Maternal age over 35

B. Previous history of cesarean section

C. Nulliparity (never having given birth)

Q5: In providing care to a pregnant woman from a different cultural background, the nurse should prioritize:

A. Imposing the nurse's own cultural beliefs and practices on the patient

B. Collaborating with an interpreter for effective communication

C. Avoiding discussions about cultural differences to prevent misunderstandings

Q6: Which factor is known to contribute to male infertility?

A. Advanced paternal age

B. Multiparity

C. Postdates gestation

Q7: Which lab value is associated with the physiologic changes in pregnancy?

A. Increased serum estrogen levels

B. Decreased serum chg. levels

C. Elevated serum creatinine levels

Q8 As a nurse attending to pregnant individuals, you come across a case with antepartum risk factors. Can you identify which factor is linked to an increased likelihood of placenta previa?

A. Adolescent pregnancy

B. Multiparity

C. Postdates gestation

Q9: Which of the following methods is commonly used for fetal assessment during pregnancy?

A. Umbilical cord blood sampling

B. Amniocentesis

C. Non-stress test

D. Chorionic villus sampling

Q10: Women who have undergone bariatric surgery and are planning a pregnancy should be aware of the potential effects on fetal development. Which of the following statements regarding bariatric surgery and fetal development is correct?

A. Bariatric surgery increases the risk of fetal growth restriction.

B. Bariatric surgery has no impact on fetal development.

C. Bariatric surgery reduces the risk of congenital anomalies.

Q11: In the assessment of fetal well-being during labor, fetal blood gases can provide valuable information about the oxygenation and acid-base status of the fetus. Which parameter is primarily used to assess fetal oxygenation?

A. pH

B. PaCO2

C. HCO3-

Q12: Fetal heart rate abnormalities can provide valuable information about the well-being of the fetus during labor. Which fetal heart rate pattern is characterized by repetitive, abrupt, and transient decreases in the baseline fetal heart rate?

A. Tachycardia

B. Bradycardia

C. Decelerations

Q13: A postpartum woman expresses concern about experiencing heavy bleeding after childbirth. Which of the following statements accurately describes postpartum hemorrhage (PPH) and its management?

A. Postpartum hemorrhage is defined as excessive bleeding after childbirth, typically exceeding 500 mL of blood loss. It can be managed by administering uterotonic medications, initiating immediate blood transfusion, and performing a manual removal of the placenta if necessary.

B. Postpartum hemorrhage rarely happens and is not common among most women. However, if it does occur, we can manage it by encouraging the woman to rest and stay hydrated, as excessive activity and dehydration can contribute to bleeding.

C Postpartum hemorrhage is uncommon and not usually expected during the postpartum period for most women, and it generally does not require any intervention. However, in some cases where the bleeding exceeds 1,000 mL, we may need to take action and consider surgical intervention to address the issue.

Q14: A postpartum woman complains of shortness of breath and chest pain. On auscultation, the nurse detects crackles in the lung fields. Which physiological change during the postpartum period is likely contributing to these symptoms?

A. Decreased blood volume

B. Increased lung capacity

C. Decreased cardiac output

Q15: A postpartum woman complains of persistent leg pain, swelling, and warmth. The nurse suspects the possibility of deep vein thrombosis (DVT). Which physiological change during the postpartum period is likely contributing to these symptoms?

A. Increased platelet count

B. Decreased blood volume

C. Increased clotting factors

Q16: A postpartum woman mentions that she is facing issues with urinary incontinence during activities like coughing, sneezing, or lifting heavy objects. What kind of urinary incontinence is probably affecting this woman?

A. Stress incontinence

B. Urge incontinence

C. Overflow incontinence

Q17: A postpartum woman presents with complaints of persistent abdominal distension and discomfort. On assessment, you observe that her abdomen is distended and tense, and she reports infrequent bowel movements. She had an uncomplicated vaginal delivery three days ago. What could be the primary reason for the woman's symptoms?

A. Postpartum constipation

B. Postpartum hemorrhage

C. Postpartum uterine atony

Q18: A postpartum woman reports having frequent loose stools since giving birth. She is concerned about this change in bowel habits. What is the most appropriate nursing response?

A. "Loose stools are a common occurrence after childbirth and will likely resolve on their own."

B. "This may be a sign of an infection, and we should have it evaluated."

C. "Have you made any recent changes in your diet that could be causing this?"

Q19: With autosomal dominant inheritance, if only one parent carries the defective gene, what is each child's chance of developing the disease?

A. 25%

B. 50%

C. 75%

Q20: A predisposing factor for assisted delivery (forceps or vacuum) is:

A. Adolescent pregnancy

B. Multiparity

C. Postdates gestation

Q21: On the second day after giving birth via cesarean delivery, a postpartum woman develops a fever. Upon assessment, the nurse notes increased uterine tenderness, foul-smelling lochia, and a heart rate of 110 beats per minute. Which condition should the nurse suspect?

A. Endometritis

B. Postpartum depression

C. Urinary tract infection

Q22: During the postpartum assessment of a woman who had a vaginal delivery, the nurse notices redness, warmth, and tenderness in one leg. The woman also complains of pain in the affected area. Which condition should the nurse suspect?

A. Deep vein thrombosis (DVT)

B. Mastitis

C. Postpartum hemorrhage

Q23: Which medication is commonly administered to prevent Rh isoimmunization in Rh-negative women during pregnancy?

A. Insulin

B. Analgesics (Tylenol)

C. Rh Immune Globulin (RhoGAM)

Q24: Which medication is commonly administered to manage postpartum depression in women?

A. Insulin

B. Analgesics (Tylenol)

C. Psychotropic Drugs

Q25: Q25: As a newborn is delivered by an HIV-positive mother which medication is usually administered to the baby to provide perinatal antiretroviral prophylaxis?

A. Insulin

B. Antiretroviral

C. Antimicrobials

Q26: A postpartum woman who is taking a daily oral contraceptive birth control pill for contraception informs the nurse that she has been prescribed an antibiotic for a urinary tract infection. What potential drug interaction should the nurse be aware of in this situation?

A. Insulin

B. Analgesics (Tylenol)

C. Antimicrobials

Q27: A postpartum woman is prescribed antihypertensive medication to manage her blood pressure. The nurse is providing patient teaching about the medication. Which instruction should the nurse include in the teaching?

A. "It is important to stop taking the medication once your blood pressure returns to normal."

B. "Take the medication at the same time each day to maintain a consistent therapeutic level."

C. "Avoid consuming foods rich in potassium while on this medication."

Q28: A postpartum woman has been prescribed analgesics (Tylenol) to manage her pain after a cesarean birth. The nurse is providing patient teaching about the medication. Which statement by the woman indicates an understanding of the teaching?

A: " "I will make sure not to take any other pain relievers from the store while I'm using Tylenol."

B: "I was told it is safe to have some alcohol in moderation while I am taking Tylenol for pain relief."

C. "I can exceed the recommended dosage if my pain is severe."

Q29: A postpartum woman complains of severe headache that worsens when sitting or standing and improves when lying flat. The nurse suspects the woman may be experiencing a spinal headache. What nursing intervention is appropriate for managing spinal headaches in the postpartum period?

A. Encouraging the woman to maintain a supine position

B. Administering over-the-counter pain relievers as needed

C. Assisting with a blood patch procedure as prescribed

Q30: A postpartum woman reports pain and discomfort in the perineal area due to vaginal lacerations. What nursing intervention is appropriate for managing vaginal lacerations in the postpartum period?

A. Providing ice packs to the perineal area

B. Administering oral analgesics as prescribed

C. Assisting with perineal hygiene after each voiding or bowel movement

Q31: A postpartum woman, who had a vaginal delivery, complains of discomfort and itching around the anal area. On examination, the nurse observes swollen and painful veins around the anus. What complication is the woman most likely experiencing?

A. Hemorrhoids

B. Afterpains

C. Breast engorgement

Q32: A postpartum woman is concerned about her nutritional needs while breastfeeding. Which statement by the woman indicates a need for further education?

A. "I should include foods rich in iron and calcium in my diet."

B. "I can continue to take my prenatal vitamins while breastfeeding."

C. "I should avoid drinking coffee and caffeinated beverages."

Q33: A postpartum woman is experiencing perineal pain and discomfort following a vaginal delivery. Which self-care measure should the nurse recommend to promote comfort and healing?

A. Using warm sits baths several times a day.

B. Applying ice packs directly to the perineal area.

C. Performing Kegel exercises multiple times a day.

Q34: A lactating mother asks about the anatomy and physiology of lactation. Which statement by the mother indicates a need for further education?

A. "The production of breast milk is primarily controlled by the hormone oxytocin."

B. "Breast milk is produced in the lobes and stored in the milk ducts within the breast."

C. "The let-down reflex is triggered by the baby's sucking, releasing milk from the alveoli."

Q35: A lactating mother expresses concern about the nutritional needs during breastfeeding. Which statement by the mother indicates a need for further education?

A. "I should include a variety of nutritious foods in my diet to ensure a good milk supply."

B. "It is important to consume extra calories and drink plenty of fluids while breastfeeding."

C. "I should avoid certain foods, such as spicy or gassy foods, to prevent discomfort in my baby."

Q36: A new mother is learning about the normal breastfeeding process. Which factor plays a crucial role in ensuring a comfortable and effective breastfeeding experience for both the mother and the baby?

A. Positioning

B. Latch On

C. Suck/Swallow Sequence

Q37: A lactation consultant is educating a group of new mothers about feeding cues in breastfeeding. Which statement accurately describes feeding cues exhibited by a hungry newborn?

A. "The baby may turn their head and open their mouth, searching for the breast."

B. "The baby may exhibit sucking motions or bring their hand to their mouth."

C. ""All of the above."

Q38: A lactating mother is concerned about low milk supply and wants to improve her milk production. The nurse recommends implementing feeding cues as part of her breastfeeding routine. How do feeding cues contribute to normal hand expression and milk production?

A. "Feeding cues help stimulate the release of oxytocin, which promotes milk ejection and effective hand expression."

B. "Feeding cues primarily influence the infant's feeding behavior and have minimal impact on hand expression or milk production."

C. "Feeding cues play a limited role in hand expression and milk production, but they are crucial for establishing a strong bond between the mother and the baby."

Q39: Sarah, a breastfeeding mother, is concerned about maintaining her milk supply while returning to work. The nurse provides education on breast care and discusses the key point of expressing and storing breast milk. Which aspect of breast care should the nurse highlight to address Sarah's concern?

A. Use of Supplementary Feedings

B. Use of Breastfeeding Devices

C. Expressing and Storing Breast Milk

Q40: A breastfeeding mother is concerned about her milk supply and asks for guidance on increasing it. The nurse provides education on breast care and emphasizes the key point of using supplementary feedings. Which aspect of breast care should the nurse focus on to address the mother's concern?

A. Use of Supplementary Feedings

B. Use of Breastfeeding Devices

C. Expressing and Storing Breast Milk

Q41: A breastfeeding mother is experiencing cracked and sore nipples. Which key point of nipple care should be recommended to promote healing and prevent further damage?

A. Applying cold compresses after each feeding

B. Using breast shells to protect the nipples

C. Expressing and storing breast milk for feedings

Q42: A breastfeeding mother has been diagnosed with a severe case of mastitis, characterized by a localized breast infection and inflammation What condition or factor would prevent breastfeeding in this situation?

A. Maternal complications

B. Latch-on problems

C. Infection/Mastitis

Q43: As a postpartum woman is undergoing treatment for a chronic medical condition that involves taking medications incompatible with breastfeeding, which of the following would make breastfeeding not advisable in this situation?

A. Insufficient milk supply

B. Therapeutic medications

C. Maternal illness

Q44: A postpartum mother expresses concern about the need for her newborn to receive phototherapy due to jaundice. The nurse explains that during the phototherapy sessions, the mother can:

A. Continue breastfeeding

B. Engage in kangaroo care

C. Limit the newborn's fluid intake

Q45: A mother has given birth to twins. The nurse is assessing the newborns for complications associated with multiple births. Which complication is commonly seen in twins and requires close monitoring?

A. Hyperbilirubinemia

B. Hypoglycemia

C. Prematurity

Q46: A term newborn is exhibiting signs of respiratory distress shortly after delivery. The nurse suspects respiratory distress syndrome What factor increases the likelihood of newborns developing respiratory distress syndrome?

A. Maternal hypertension

B. Maternal diabetes

C. Maternal age over 35

Q47: Which behavior is considered a normal characteristic of new parents bonding with their newborn?

A. Showing minimal interest in holding and cuddling the baby

B. Exhibiting a strong desire for alone time without the baby

C. Engaging in frequent eye contact, talking, and soothing the baby

Q48: A postpartum nurse is providing education to a group of new mothers about the benefits of rooming-in with their newborns. The nurse explains that rooming-in promotes normal infant interactions and enhances maternal-infant bonding. Which of the following statements accurately describes rooming-in?

A. "Rooming-in allows you to have your baby stay in the nursery for the majority of the day."

B. "Rooming-in involves keeping your baby in a separate room away from your bedside."

C. "Rooming-in encourages keeping your baby with you in the same room throughout the day and night."

49: A postpartum nurse is conducting a discharge teaching session for a woman who experienced a cesarean birth. The nurse discusses the importance of self-care and provides guidance on activities to promote healing and recovery. Which statement made by the woman indicates the need for further education regarding self-care after a cesarean birth?

A. "I will be careful to avoid any heavy lifting for at least six weeks."

B. "I should take short, frequent walks to aid in circulation and prevent blood clots."

C. "I will apply warm compresses to my incision to reduce pain and promote healing."

Q50: A postpartum nurse is providing support to a woman who is experiencing postpartum depression PPD. The nurse understands that PPD can have an impact on the woman is ability to care for her newborn and her older children. Which intervention would be most appropriate for the nurse to implement to support the woman and her family?

A. Encouraging the woman to isolate herself from her family until she feels better.

B. Collaborating with the woman's healthcare provider to adjust her medication without her knowledge.

C. Assisting the woman in accessing community resources and support groups for postpartum depression.

Q51: A postpartum nurse is caring for a woman who is experiencing postpartum depression PPD. The nurse recognizes that PPD can have significant effects on parent/infant interactions. Which statement accurately describes the impact of PPD on parent/infant interactions?

A. "PPD often leads to increased positive interactions between the parent and the infant."

B. "Infants of mothers with PPD may have difficulty forming secure attachments."

Q52: A postpartum nurse is assessing a family's readiness for discharge and identifies limited social support as a potential barrier to successful family integration. Which intervention would be most appropriate to address this barrier?

A. Referring the family to local parenting classes and support groups.

B. Encouraging the family to rely solely on their immediate family members for support.

C. Advising the family to avoid seeking outside assistance to foster independence.

Q53: A postpartum nurse is providing education on cultural factors affecting family integration to a group of healthcare professionals. The nurse emphasizes the importance of cultural sensitivity and awareness. Which statement accurately reflects the impact of cultural sensitivity on family integration?

A. "Cultural sensitivity is not relevant to family integration and should be disregarded."

B. "Cultural sensitivity can enhance communication and understanding within culturally diverse families."

C. "Cultural sensitivity may lead to misunderstandings and should be avoided in healthcare settings."

Q54 A postpartum nurse is conducting a routine assessment on a postpartum woman and suspects intimate partner violence. Which action would be most appropriate for the nurse to take?

A. Ignore the suspicion unless the woman discloses the abuse voluntarily.

B. Document the findings and discuss them with the healthcare team.

C. Confront the woman's partner directly about the suspected abuse.

Q55: In a postpartum education session, a nurse is discussing the importance of family planning with a group of new mothers. One mother asks about the most effective method of contraception while breastfeeding. Which response by the nurse is most accurate and helpful?

A. "Using condoms or other barrier methods of contraception are the safest options while breastfeeding."

B. "You should avoid all forms of hormonal contraception as they can interfere with breast milk production."

C. "Intrauterine devices IUDs are safe and highly effective for breastfeeding mothers looking for long-acting reversible contraceptives."

Q56: A nurse is providing education to a couple who has chosen open adoption for their newborn. Which statement by the nurse accurately describes open adoption?

A. "Open adoption allows for ongoing contact and communication between the birth parents, adoptive parents, and the child."

B. "Open adoption means that the birth parents have no involvement or contact with the child once the adoption is finalized."

C. "Open adoption involves temporary placement of the child with the birth parents for a specified period before permanent adoption occurs."

Q57: A couple is experiencing perinatal grief following a miscarriage. Which statement by the nurse is most appropriate to validate their feelings and provide support?

A. "Miscarriage is a common occurrence, and you'll have another chance to conceive soon."

B. "I understand how devastating this loss is for you. Grieving is a normal and individual process."

C. "You should try to focus on the future and not dwell on what has happened."

Q58: A couple is considering home birth for their upcoming delivery. They express concerns about the availability of emergency medical interventions in case of complications. Which ethical principle should guide the nurse's response?

A. Autonomy

B. Beneficence

C. Nonmaleficence

Q59: A newborn is found to have a high-pitched cry, seizures, and feeding difficulties. What condition should the nurse suspect?

A. Hypoglycemia

B. Hyperbilirubinemia

C. Neonatal abstinence syndrome

Q60: A newborn's umbilical cord has two arteries and one vein. What is the normal composition of umbilical vessels?

A. Two veins and two arteries

B. One vein and one artery

C. Two arteries and one vein

Q61: A term newborn is experiencing cold stress. Which physiological response is commonly associated with cold stress in newborns?

A. Bradycardia

B. Hyperglycemia

C. Decreased respiratory rate

Q62: A nurse is assessing a newborn's blood gas values. Which finding would suggest respiratory acidosis?

A. pH of 7.50

B. PaCO2 of 25 mmHg

C. HCO3- of 22 me/L

Q63: A newborn is suspected to have an infection. Which laboratory test would be most useful in identifying the causative organism?

A. Complete blood count CBC

B. Blood culture

C. Urinalysis

Q64: A nurse is performing a gestational age assessment on a newborn using the Dubowitz/Ballard Assessment. Which finding would suggest a newborn to be at term?

A. Flat areolae without buds

B. Thin, wrinkled skin

C. Soft, flexible ear cartilage

Q65: A newborn is suspected to be small for gestational age (SGA). Which assessment finding would support this suspicion?

A. Overlapping cranial sutures

B. Fused labia majora

C. Absent plantar creases

Q66: A nurse is assessing a newborn's neurological function using the Brazelton Neonatal Behavioral Assessment Scale (NBAS). Which behavior would be considered abnormal?

A. Clenching of fists

B. Grasping of objects

C. Turning head in response to sound D.

Q67: During a neurobehavioral assessment, a newborn demonstrates a strong startle response when a loud noise is made. What is this response called?

A. Moro reflex

B. Babinski reflex

C. Tonic neck reflex

Q68: A normal finding of male genitalia in the term neonate is:

A. Retractable prepuce

B. Rugatescrotum

C. Testes in the inguinal canal

Q69: A new mother asks the nurse about when the umbilical cord stump will fall off her newborn. How should the nurse respond?

A. "The cord stump usually falls off within 24 hours after birth."

B. "The cord stump typically falls off within 1 to 2 weeks after birth."

C. "The cord stump usually falls off within 4 to 6 weeks after birth."

Q70: A parent asks the nurse about the frequency of diaper changes for a newborn. What is the nurse's best response?

A. "Newborns typically need their diapers changed every 4 to 6 hours."

B. "It is recommended to change the diaper every time the newborn passes urine or stool."

C. "Diaper changes can be done every 8 to 12 hours to promote skin integrity."

Q71: A nurse is preparing to perform a circumcision on a newborn. Which intervention should the nurse prioritize to ensure the newborn's safety?

A. Administering pain medication prior to the procedure.

B. Applying a sterile dressing to the circumcision site.

C. Placing the newborn in a supine position with appropriate restraints.

Q72: A nurse is providing education to new parents about pain management during procedures for their newborn. Which statement by the parents indicates understanding of comfort measures?

A. "We can apply a numbing cream before vaccinations to reduce pain."

B. "We should avoid holding our newborn during blood tests to prevent distress."

C. "We can give our newborn a bottle of formula during painful procedures to provide comfort."

Q73: A newborn is experiencing difficulty falling asleep. Which comfort measure should the nurse recommend to promote sleep?

A. Dimming the lights and minimizing noise in the environment

B. Engaging in vigorous play to tire out the newborn

C. Applying a warm heating pad to the newborn's crib

Q74: A nurse is educating parents about the importance of CHD screening for newborns. What should the nurse include as a potential benefit of early detection?

A. Timely initiation of treatment and intervention for CHD

B. Increased breastfeeding success rates in newborns

C. Prevention of common newborn infections

Q75: A parent asks the nurse about the optimal timing for CHD screening in their newborn. What is the nurse's best response?

A. "CHD screening is typically performed within 24 to 48 hours after birth."

B. "CHD screening is done during the newborn's first routine check-up, usually around 4 to 6 weeks of age."

C. "CHD screening is not necessary unless there are visible signs or symptoms of heart problems."

Q76: A nurse is providing education to parents about newborn skin care. Which statement by the parents indicates understanding of skin care practices?

A. "We should use mild, fragrance-free cleansers for bathing our newborn."

B. "It's important to vigorously rub the newborn's skin to dry it completely after bathing."

C. "We can use adult moisturizers and lotions on our newborn's skin."

Q77: A parent asks the nurse about managing cradle cap in their newborn. What is the nurse's best response?

A. "Gently massage the newborn's scalp with mineral oil to loosen the scales, then wash with a mild baby shampoo."

B. "Scrub the newborn's scalp vigorously with a washcloth to remove the scales."

C. "Apply an over-the-counter antifungal cream to the affected areas of the scalp."

Q78: A nurse is discussing safe sleep environments with parents. Which item should the nurse advise against having in the newborn's sleep area?

A. Stuffed animals

B. Firm mattress

C. Sleep sack or wearable blanket

Q79: A parent asks the nurse about the recommended room temperature for their newborn's sleep environment. What is the nurse's best response?

A. "Maintain a comfortable room temperature between 68 to 72 degrees Fahrenheit 20 to 22 degrees Celsius."

B. "Keep the room warm to prevent your newborn from getting cold during sleep."

C. "Room temperature is not a concern for newborns during sleep."

Q80: A nurse is preparing to administer vaccines and immunoglobulins to a newborn. Which vaccine is routinely given to newborns to prevent hepatitis B?

A. DTaP Diphtheria, Tetanus, Pertussis vaccine

B. MMR Measles, Mumps, Rubella vaccine

C. Hepatitis B vaccine

Q81: A newborn is receiving eye prophylaxis shortly after birth. What is the purpose of administering eye prophylaxis to a newborn?

A. To prevent conjunctivitis and eye infections caused by certain bacteria

B. To promote eye development and visual acuity in the newborn

C. To reduce eye inflammation and itching in the newborn

Q82: A newborn is born with a heart rate of less than hundred beats per minute despite adequate ventilation. What intervention should be performed?

A. Administer epinephrine intravenously

B. Administer normal saline bolus

C. Initiate chest compressions

Q83: A newborn is born with gasping respirations and a heart rate of less than sixty beats per minute. What is the most appropriate intervention?

A. Administer positive-pressure ventilation with 100% oxygen

B. Administer chest compressions

C. Initiate endotracheal intubation

Q84: What is the primary goal of providing positive-pressure ventilation during newborn resuscitation?

A. Maintaining oxygenation

B. Establishing effective circulation

C. Clearing the airway of meconium

Q85: If the heart rate of a newborn is less than 60 beats per minute after 30 seconds of positive-pressure ventilation, what intervention should be initiated?

A. Administering chest compressions

B. Performing endotracheal intubation

C. Administering epinephrine intravenously

Q86: What medication is typically administered to newborns as eye prophylaxis to prevent ophthalmia neonatorum?

A. Erythromycin ointment

B. Acyclovir cream

C. Gentamicin drops

Q87: Which medication is commonly used for pain management in newborns undergoing procedures?

A. Lidocaine

B. Fentanyl

C. Acetaminophen

Q88: A newborn with suspected sepsis was started on intravenous antibiotics. Which assessment finding suggests that the treatment is effective?

A. Increased temperature

B. Worsening respiratory distress

C. Improved general appearance

Q89: A newborn with hypoglycemia was given a glucose infusion. What finding indicates the effectiveness of the intervention?

A. Increased irritability

B. Decreased blood glucose levels

C. Improved feeding tolerance

Q90: What is the maximum score a newborn can receive on the Apgar scale?

A. 5

B. 7

C. 10

Q91: A newborn scores 3 on the Apgar scale at 1 minute after birth. What action should be taken?

A. Immediate resuscitation is needed.

B. The newborn is in fair condition and should be closely monitored.

C. The score is within the normal range, no further action is required.

Q92: What increases the chances of experiencing postpartum hemorrhage?

A. Multiparity

B. Cesarean birth

C. Preterm delivery

Q93: The first-line treatment for postpartum hemorrhage due to uterine atony is:

A. Oxytocin

B. Methylergonovine

C. Misoprostol

Q94: What symptom is often linked to postpartum thrombophlebitis?

A. Redness and warmth over the affected area

B. Numbness and tingling in the extremities

C. Severe headache and blurred vision

Q95: The nurse should instruct the postpartum woman with thrombophlebitis to:

A. Elevate the affected extremity

B. Apply heat to the affected area

C. Massage the clot to promote blood flow

Q96: The most appropriate diagnostic test to confirm the presence of thrombophlebitis is:

A. Ultrasound

B. Magnetic resonance imaging MRI

C. X-ray

Q97: What factor raises the risk of developing a pulmonary embolus after childbirth?

A. Cesarean birth

B. Maternal age over 40

C. Gestational diabetes

Q98: The classic signs and symptoms of pulmonary embolus include:

A. Sudden onset of chest pain and shortness of breath

B. Abdominal pain and bloating

C. Headache and dizziness

Q99: The primary pathophysiological process in DIC involves:

A. Excessive activation of the coagulation system

B. Impaired platelet function

C. Inadequate production of clotting factors

Q100: Clinical manifestations of DIC may include:

A. Petechiae and ecchymosis

B. Hypertension and edema

C. Constipation and abdominal pain

Q101: The clinical manifestations of HELLP syndrome may include:

A. Abdominal pain Nausea and Vomiting

B. Joint pain, Fatigue, and Weight gain

C. Headache, Visual disturbances, and Epigastric pain

Q102: Laboratory findings consistent with HELLP syndrome include:

A. Decreased hemoglobin and hematocrit levels

B. Elevated liver enzymes (AST, ALT)

C. Increased platelet count

Q103: The nursing management of a perineal hematoma involves:

A. Applying ice packs to reduce swelling

B. Administering pain medication as prescribed

C. Monitoring vital signs and assessing for signs of infection

Q104: A woman with a perineal hematoma may require:

A. Surgical drainage

B. Antibiotic therapy

C. Bed rest and elevation of the affected area

Q105: Risk factors for the development of a perineal hematoma include:

A. Episiotomy

B. Prolonged second stage of labor

C. Maternal age over 35

Q106: Which of the following medications is commonly used to manage chronic hypertension during pregnancy?

A. Nonsteroidal anti-inflammatory drugs NSAIDs

B. Angiotensin-converting enzyme (ACE) inhibitors

C. Methyldopa

Q107: Maternal complications associated with chronic hypertension include:

A. Deep vein thrombosis

B. Cardiac arrhythmias

C. Stroke

Q108: Women with chronic hypertension should be advised to:

A. Limit their sodium intake

B. Avoid physical activity

C. Stop taking their antihypertensive medication

Q109: Gestational hypertension is characterized by blood pressure measurements of:

A. ≥140/90 mmHg on two occasions at least 4 hours apart

B. ≥130/80 mmHg on two occasions at least 6 hours apart

C. ≥120/80 mmHg on two occasions at least 8 hours apart

Q110: The most effective treatment for gestational hypertension is:

A. Bed rest

B. Antihypertensive medication

C. Increased fluid intake

Q111: The most common initial symptom of eclampsia is:

A. Severe headache

B. Visual disturbances

C. Epigastric pain

Q112: Eclampsia is a medical emergency that requires immediate:

A. Administration of anticoagulants

B. Delivery of the fetus

C. Initiation of corticosteroid therapy

Q113: Risk factors for developing endometritis include:

A. Prolonged rupture of membranes

B. Primiparity

C. Preterm birth

Q114: Clinical manifestations of endometritis include:

A. Fever

B. Vaginal bleeding

C. Hypotension

Q115: The most common causative organisms of postpartum wound infections are:

A. staphylococcus aureus or Streptococcus pyogenes are the two options to choose from.

B. Escherichia coli or Klebsiella pneumoniae

C. Group B Streptococcus or Enterococcus faecalis

Q116: The recommended treatment for a postpartum wound infection includes:

A. Antibiotics

B. Warm compresses

C. Topical antifungal cream

Q117: Women with a postpartum wound infection may experience:

A. Fever

B. Increased uterine bleeding

C. Constipation

Q118: The most common causative organism of septic pelvic thrombophlebitis is:

A. Streptococcus pyogenes

B. Escherichia coli

C. Staphylococcus aureus

Q119: The recommended treatment for septic pelvic thrombophlebitis includes:

A. Intravenous antibiotics

B. Anticoagulation therapy

C. Surgical drainage of abscesses

Q120: Women with septic pelvic thrombophlebitis may experience:

A. High-grade fever

B. Rapid heart rate

C. Hypotension

Q121: The recommended treatment for postpartum UTIs includes:

A. Antibiotic therapy

B. Fluid hydration

C. Pelvic rest

Q122: Women with postpartum UTIs may experience:

A. Fever and chills

B. Hematuria (blood in urine)

C. Hypotension

Q123: The most important nursing intervention for a woman with a postpartum UTI is:

A. Encouraging adequate fluid intake

B. Administering prescribed antibiotics

C. Providing perineal care

Q124: The initial screening test for gestational diabetes is typically performed during which trimester of pregnancy?

A. First trimester

B. Second trimester

C. Third trimester

Q125: The gold standard diagnostic test for gestational diabetes is:

A. Fasting plasma glucose test

B. Oral glucose tolerance test (OGTT)

C. Glycosylated hemoglobin HbA1c test

Q126: Women experiencing postpartum sleep disturbances should be advised to avoid:

A. Napping during the day

B. Establishing a bedtime routine

C. Using electronic devices before bed

Q127: What is the recommended duration for daytime napping to help alleviate postpartum sleep disturbances?

A. 15-30 minutes

B. 45-60 minutes

C. 90-120 minutes

Q128: Postpartum women with sleep disturbances can benefit from implementing good sleep hygiene practices. Which of the following is a sleep hygiene recommendation?

A. Engaging in stimulating activities before bed

B. Consuming a large meal close to bedtime

C. Creating a quiet and comfortable sleep environment

Q129: The Edinburgh Postnatal Depression Scale EPDS is a commonly used screening tool for postpartum depression. What is the recommended cutoff score on the EPDS that indicates further assessment is necessary?

A. 5

B. 10

C. 15

Q130: When assessing a woman for postpartum depression it is important to differentiate between "baby blues" and clinical depression. How long does "baby blues" typically last?

A. 24 hours

B. 1 week

C. 2-3 weeks

Q131: A woman with postpartum psychosis may exhibit signs of confusion, agitation, and disorientation. What is the most appropriate initial nursing intervention in this situation?

A. Administering an antipsychotic medication

B. Placing the woman in a quiet and safe environment

C. Encouraging social interaction and engagement

Q132: Maternal substance abuse can lead to neonatal abstinence syndrome (NAS) in the newborn. Which of the following substances is commonly associated with NAS?

A. Caffeine

B. Antidepressants

C. Opioids

Q133: When caring for a pregnant woman with substance use disorder the primary goal is to ensure the health and wellbeing of both the mother or the fetus. Which of the following interventions is a priority?

A. Implementing punitive measures to discourage substance use

B. Encouraging the woman to quit substance use immediately

C. Providing non-judgmental support, education, and access to treatment resources

Q134: One common type of cyanotic heart disease is Tetralogy of Fallot Which of the following features is associated with Tetralogy of Fallot?

A. A hole in the wall separating the two ventricles

B. Narrowing of the aorta

C. Displacement of the aorta to the right

Q135: Newborns with cyanotic heart disease may present with cyanosis, but the severity can vary. What factors can lead to more cyanosis in newborns with cyanotic heart disease?

A. Feeding difficulties

B. Exposure to cold temperature

C. High humidity

Q136: The nursing management of a newborn with cyanotic heart disease includes monitoring for signs of inadequate oxygenation. Which of the following signs may indicate inadequate oxygenation in a newborn with cyanotic heart disease?

A. Increased heart rate

B. Decreased respiratory rate

C. Pink skin color

Q137: A newborn with a cyanotic heart disease presents with tachypnea, poor feeding, and failure to thrive. Which of the following a cyanotic heart defects is commonly associated with these symptoms?

A. Atrial septal defect (ASD)

B. Coarctation of the aorta

C. Patent ductus arteriosus (PDA)

Q138: A nurse is caring for a preterm newborn who is experiencing apnea. Which of the following interventions is appropriate for managing apnea in preterm infants?

A. Administering supplemental oxygen during episodes of apnea.

B. Administering sedatives to promote relaxation and decrease respiratory effort.

C. Placing the newborn in a prone position to improve breathing.

Q139: A nurse is caring for a newborn with suspected Transient Tachypnea of the Newborn (TTN). Which of the following clinical manifestations is commonly observed in infants with TTN?

A. Bradycardia and cyanosis

B. Hypotension and low blood sugar levels

C. Rapid breathing and grunting sounds

Q140: A nurse is assessing a newborn for signs of pneumothorax. What signs or symptoms are frequently linked to pneumothorax in newborns?

A. Bradycardia and hypotension

B. Rapid breathing and cyanosis

C. Low body temperature and poor feeding

Q141: A nurse is assessing a newborn for signs of meconium aspiration. Which of the following clinical manifestations is commonly associated with meconium aspiration syndrome?

A. Cyanosis and respiratory distress

B. Jaundice and poor feeding

C. Bradycardia and low body temperature

Q142: A nurse is caring for a newborn who is experiencing seizures. What are some signs or symptoms that could suggest seizures in a newborn?

A. Jerking or stiffening movements

B. Excessive sleepiness and lethargy

C. Poor feeding and weight loss

Q143: A nurse is assessing a newborn who is experiencing jitteriness. Which of the following clinical manifestations may be observed in a newborn with jitteriness?

A. Excessive sleepiness and decreased responsiveness

B. Increased appetite and weight gain

C. Rapid breathing and irritability

Q144: s a nurse caring for a newborn suspected of having intracranial hemorrhage what signs might be observed in the newborn?

A. Excessive sleepiness and decreased responsiveness

B. Increased appetite and weight gain

C. Absence of any noticeable changes in behavior or appearance

Q145: A nurse is providing prenatal education to a pregnant woman about neural tube defects. How does folic acid help prevent neural tube defects?

A. Taking folic acid supplements is crucial throughout the entire pregnancy to ensure the prevention of neural tube defects.

B. " To reduce the risk of neural tube defect it is recommended to take folic acid supplements consistently throughout pregnancy.

C. "Folic acid supplementation has no effect on the prevention of neural tube defects."

Q146: A pregnant woman with a history of substance abuse is admitted to the labor and delivery unit. The nurse knows that substance abuse during pregnancy increases the risk of which gastrointestinal complication in the newborn?

A. Necrotizing enterocolitis

B. Gastroesophageal reflux

C. Meconium ileus

Q147: A nurse is caring for a newborn with an imperforate anus. Which of the following actions should the nurse prioritize in the immediate care of this newborn?

A. Assessing for signs of meconium passage

B. Administering intravenous fluids to maintain hydration

C. Initiating nasogastric tube insertion for decompression

Q148: A newborn is diagnosed with omphalocele. Which of the following statements accurately describes this condition?

A. It is a protrusion of abdominal contents through a defect in the abdominal wall near the umbilicus.

B. It is an abnormal opening in the diaphragm, allowing abdominal organs to herniate into the chest cavity.

C. It is a failure of the intestines to return to the abdominal cavity during fetal development.

Q149: A newborn is diagnosed with Rh incompatibility. Which intervention is a priority in the care of this newborn?

A. Administering Rh immune globulin (RhoGAM) to the mother

B. Initiating phototherapy to prevent hyperbilirubinemia

C. Monitoring the newborn's blood glucose levels

Q150: A newborn is diagnosed with late-onset vitamin K deficiency bleeding (VKDB). Which statement accurately describes late-onset VKDB?

A. It typically occurs within the first 24 hours after birth.

B. It is primarily caused by maternal vitamin K deficiency.

C. It can present as bleeding from various sites, such as the gastrointestinal tract or intracranially.

Q151: A nurse is providing education to parents about vitamin K administration to their newborn. Which statement by the parents indicates understanding of the information?

A. "We should give our baby vitamin K drops every day for the first month."

B. "The vitamin K injection is painful for the baby but necessary."

C. "We can rely on the vitamin K present in breast milk to meet our baby's needs."

Q152: A nurse is assessing a newborn with hyperbilirubinemia. Which physical finding is associated with severe hyperbilirubinemia?

A. Kernicterus

B. Caput succedaneum

C. Milia

Q153: A newborn with ABO incompatibility may present with which clinical manifestation?

A. Jaundice

B. Respiratory distress

C. Petechiae

Q154: How can ABO incompatibility in a newborn be managed?

A. Phototherapy

B. Exchange transfusion

C. Supportive care

Q155: Which blood type is at the highest risk for developing hemolytic disease of the newborn due to Rh incompatibility?

A. O positive

B. A positive

C. AB positive

Q156: What is the recommended management for infants with G6PD deficiency?

A. Avoidance of triggers

B. Blood transfusion

C. Iron supplementation

Q157: Which of the following substances can trigger hemolysis in individuals with G6PD deficiency?

A. Antibiotics

B. Anticoagulants

C. Antihypertensive medications

Q158: When assessing a newborn for polycythemia, the nurse should prioritize which diagnostic test?

A. Complete blood count (CBC)

B. Blood culture

C. Blood glucose level

Q159: Which intervention should the nurse prioritize to prevent complications in a neonate with polycythemia?

A. Administering intravenous fluids

B. Performing frequent blood transfusions

C. Monitoring for signs of respiratory distress

Q160: A nurse is caring for a neonate with hyper viscosity. Which clinical manifestation should the nurse monitor for as a potential complication?

A. Petechiae and ecchymosis

B. Hypotension and bradycardia

C. Hypothermia and poor weight gain

Q161: A nurse is caring for a neonate with thrombocytopenia. Which clinical manifestation should the nurse monitor for as a potential complication?

A. Petechiae and purpura

B. Hypertension and tachycardia

C. Hyperthermia and diaphoresis

Q162: A nurse is caring for a neonate with suspected neonatal sepsis. Which clinical manifestation should the nurse monitor for as a potential sign of sepsis?

A. Hypotension and bradycardia

B. Rapid breathing and respiratory distress

C. Jaundice and abnormal liver function tests

Q163: When interpreting the results of a neonatal CBC and differential, the nurse notes an increased percentage of neutrophils. What does this finding suggest?

A. Bacterial infection

B. Viral infection

C. Parasitic infection

Q164: Which of the following newborns is most likely to have an elevated WBC count on the CBC?

A. A newborn with a congenital heart defect

B. A newborn with meconium aspiration syndrome

C. A newborn with hypoglycemia

Q165: What is the primary purpose of performing a lumbar puncture in a newborn with suspected meningitis?

A. To assess CSF pressure

B. To evaluate CSF glucose level

C. To analyze CSF for presence of bacteria or viruses

Q166: Which complication should the nurse monitor for following a lumbar puncture in a newborn?

A. Increased blood pressure

B. Respiratory distress

C. Hypoglycemia

Q167: During pregnancy, a woman expresses worry about the possibility of transmitting HIV to her newborn. What recommended intervention can help lower the risk of perinatal HIV transmission?

A. Antiretroviral therapy during pregnancy

B. Administration of intravenous immunoglobulin IVIG to the newborn

C. Early induction of labor before term

Q168: A newborn is suspected to have chlamydia conjunctivitis. What intervention is recommended to prevent ophthalmia neonatorum in newborns born to mothers with chlamydia infection?

A. Administering intravenous antibiotics to the newborn

B. Applying erythromycin ointment to the newborn's eyes

C. Isolating the newborn in a separate room to prevent transmission

Q169: A newborn is diagnosed with neonatal herpes simplex virus HSV infection. Which precaution should the healthcare provider emphasize when caring for the newborn to prevent HSV transmission?

A. Wearing gloves during diaper changes

B. Placing the newborn in a separate isolation room

C. Restricting visitors from interacting with the newborn

D. Encouraging exclusive breastfeeding to boost immunity

Q170: A newborn is prescribed intravenous ampicillin for the treatment of a suspected bacterial infection. What is the primary nursing consideration when administering intravenous antibiotics to a newborn?

A. Assessing for signs of allergic reactions

B. Monitoring renal function during therapy

C. Checking for compatibility with other intravenous fluids

Q171: A newborn is diagnosed with ophthalmia neonatorum due to Chlamydia trachomatis infection. What medication is commonly used to treat this condition?

A. Erythromycin ointment

B. Acyclovir cream

C. Nystatin drops

Q172: Hypoglycemia in newborns is defined as a blood glucose level below:

A. 40 mg/dL

B. 50 mg/dL

C. 60 mg/dL

Q173: A newborn is displaying symptoms of poor feeding, vomiting, and developmental delays. The most likely cause of these symptoms is:

A. Galactosemia

B. Hypothyroidism

C. Tay-Sachs disease

Q174: In a family with autosomal dominant inheritance, what is the chance of passing on the condition to each child if one parent carries the defective gene?

A. 25%

B. 50%

C. 75%

Q175: What is the most common cause of macrosomia in infants of diabetic mothers?

A. Excessive maternal weight gain

B. Genetic factors

C. Maternal hyperglycemia

Test 2 Answer Key

1	C	26	C	51	C
2	B	27	B	52	A
3	C	28	A	53	B
4	B	29	C	54	B
5	B	30	A	55	C
6	A	31	A	56	A
7	A	32	B	57	B
8	B	33	A	58	C
9	C	34	B	59	C
10	A	35	B	60	C
11	A	36	A	61	A
12	C	37	C	62	B
13	A	38	A	63	B
14	C	39	C	64	C
15	C	40	A	65	C
16	A	41	B	66	C
17	C	42	C	67	A
18	A	43	B	68	B
19	B	44	A	69	B
20	C	45	C	70	B
21	A	46	C	71	A
22	A	47	C	72	A
23	C	48	C	73	A
24	C	49	C	74	A
25	B	50	C	75	A

76	A	102	B	128	C
77	A	103	C	129	C
78	A	104	A	130	C
79	A	105	B	131	B
80	C	106	C	132	C
81	A	107	C	133	C
82	C	108	A	134	C
83	A	109	A	135	B
84	A	110	B	136	A
85	A	111	A	137	C
86	A	112	B	138	A
87	B	113	A	139	C
88	C	114	A	140	B
89	C	115	A	141	A
90	C	116	A	142	A
91	A	117	A	143	C
92	B	118	B	144	A
93	A	119	A	145	B
94	A	120	A	146	A
95	A	121	A	147	A
96	A	122	A	148	A
97	A	123	B	149	A
98	A	124	B	150	C
99	A	125	B	151	B
100	A	126	C	152	A
101	C	127	A	153	A

154	C		**162**	B		**170**	C
155	C		**163**	A		**171**	A
156	A		**164**	B		**172**	C
157	A		**165**	C		**173**	A
158	A		**166**	B		**174**	B
159	C		**167**	A		**175**	C
160	A		**168**	B			
161	A		**169**	A			

Maternal Newborn Nursing Exam Practice Test 3

Q1 Which antenatal factor is associated with an increased risk of gestational diabetes mellitus GDM during pregnancy?

A. Advanced maternal age

B. Obesity

C. Nulliparity

Q2: The Lamaze breathing pattern begins and ends with:

A. Slow-paced breath through the mouth

B. Rapid panting breaths

C. Cleansing breaths

Q3: Adequate nutrition during pregnancy is crucial for the health and development of both the mother and the baby. Which of the following nutrients plays a key role in the formation or maintenance of the baby's bones and teeth?

A. Vitamin A

B. Vitamin C

C. Calcium

Q4: Obstetrical history is an important factor to consider in assessing pregnancy and birth risk factors. What type of obstetrical history is linked to a higher chance of preterm birth?

A. Previous history of multiple gestations

B. Advanced maternal age

C. Primiparity (first-time pregnancy)

Q5: In providing care to a pregnant woman who follows a specific cultural practice during pregnancy, the nurse should:

A. Discourage the cultural practice to promote evidence-based care

B. Respect and integrate the cultural practice into the care plan, if it is safe and does not pose harm

C. Confront the woman about the cultural practice and explain its potential negative effects

Q6: Which factor is associated with an increased risk of female infertility?

A. Early menarche

B. Multiparity

C. Postpartum depression

Q7: Which physiological change occurs during pregnancy and can affect a woman's basal metabolic rate (BMR)?

A. Decrease

B. Increase

C. Remain stable

Q8: A 28-year-old pregnant woman has a history of gestational diabetes mellitus GDM in a previous pregnancy. Which of the following antepartum risk factors is she at an increased risk for developing in her current pregnancy?

A. Preterm labor

B. Gestational hypertension

C. Recurrent GDM

Q9: Which fetal assessment method is used to evaluate the fetal heart rate response to fetal movement?

A. Biophysical profile

B. Contraction stress test

C. Non-stress test

Q10: A pregnant woman who underwent bariatric surgery two years ago is seeking advice regarding her nutritional needs during pregnancy What type of obstetrical history is linked to a higher chance of preterm birth?

A. Increase her calorie intake to support fetal growth and development.

B. Monitor her vitamin D levels regularly due to the increased risk of deficiency.

C. Consult with a registered dietitian experienced in bariatric nutrition.

Q11: Fetal heart rate patterns are important indicators of fetal well-being during labor. Which fetal heart rate pattern is characterized by repetitive late decelerations that coincide with uterine contractions?

A. Early decelerations

B. Variable decelerations

C. Accelerations

D. Prolonged decelerations

Q12: During labor, the healthcare team monitors the fetal heart rate (FHR) to assess the well-being of the baby. Which FHR pattern is characterized by a baseline heart rate below 110 beats per minute that lasts longer than 10 minutes?

A. Tachycardia

B. Bradycardia

C. Altered variability

Q13: A postpartum woman reports experiencing heavy vaginal bleeding and passing large blood clots. On examination, the healthcare provider finds the uterus to be firm and midline. What could be the most probable reason for the bleeding?

A. Retained placental fragments

B. Uterine atony

C. Cervical laceration

Q14: A postpartum woman complains of persistent shortness of breath, chest pain, and rapid breathing. The nurse suspects the possibility of a pulmonary embolism (PE). Which physiological change during the postpartum period is likely contributing to these symptoms?

A. Increased red blood cell production

B. Decreased vascular resistance

C. Decreased lung compliance

Q15: A postpartum woman complains of excessive sweating, palpitations, and heat intolerance. Which physiological change during the postpartum period is likely contributing to these symptoms?

A. Increased thyroid hormone production

B. Decreased cardiac output

C. Increased progesterone levels

D. Decreased blood volume

Q16: A postpartum woman presents with complaints of pain and discomfort in the perineal area. Upon assessment, you observe redness, swelling, and tenderness in the area. Which of the following interventions should be included in the management of this woman's condition?

A. Applying cold packs to the perineal area

B. Administering oral analgesics as needed

C. Encouraging regular sits baths

Q17: A postpartum woman presents with persistent abdominal pain and distension two days after a cesarean delivery. On physical examination, you note localized tenderness and guarding in the right lower quadrant. The woman's vital signs are stable, and she has a low-grade fever. What is the most likely cause of her symptoms?

A. Endometritis

B. Urinary tract infection

C. Appendicitis

Q18: A postpartum woman reports experiencing frequent flatulence and bloating since giving birth. She asks if this is normal. What is the most appropriate nursing response?

A. "These symptoms are common after childbirth and should subside as your body adjusts."

B. "Excessive flatulence and bloating can indicate a gastrointestinal disorder, and we should investigate further."

C. Have you made any noteworthy adjustments to your diet after giving birth?

Q19: Removing a neonate from an incubator for procedures without the use of an overhead warmer will result in heat loss by

A. convection

B. evaporation

C. radiation

Q20: During a physical assessment of a term neonate, which finding would be considered a normal finding for male genitalia?

A. Retractable prepuce

B. Rugatescrotum

C. Testes in the inguinal canal

Q21: A postpartum woman who delivered vaginally is experiencing heavy bleeding with the passage of large blood clots and a saturated perineal pad within an hour. The nurse suspects postpartum hemorrhage and initiates immediate interventions. Which intervention should the nurse prioritize?

A. Administering uterotonics

B. Performing fundal massage

C. Preparing for blood transfusion

Q22: A postpartum woman presents with signs and symptoms of mastitis, including breast redness, swelling, and tenderness. The nurse is providing education on self-care measures. Which instruction should the nurse prioritize?

A. Encouraging frequent breastfeeding or pumping

B. Applying warm compresses to the affected breast

C. Administering prescribed antibiotics as directed

Q23: A postpartum woman with a history of hypertension requires medication to manage her blood pressure. Which medication is frequently given as a blood pressure lowering drug during the postpartum period?

B. Analgesics (Tylenol)

C. Antihypertensives

Q24: A newborn is born to a mother with a history of substance use disorder and is at risk of experiencing neonatal abstinence syndrome NAS. Which medication is commonly used to manage NAS in newborns?

A. Insulin

B. Analgesics (Tylenol)

C. Methadone (Subutex)

Q25: A newborn is diagnosed with gastroesophageal reflux GER and is experiencing feeding difficulties. Which medication is commonly administered as a GI motility drug to manage GER symptoms?

A. Insulin

B. Analgesics (Tylenol)

C. GI Motility Drugs

Q26 A woman after childbirth is given an antimicrobial medication for a urinary tract infection. She informs the nurse that she is currently on an antihypertensive medication to manage her high blood pressure. What potential drug interaction should the nurse be aware of in this situation?

A. Antimicrobials

B. Antihypertensives

C. Insulin

Q27: A postpartum woman is prescribed antihypertensive medication for high blood pressure. Which statement by the woman indicates understanding of the medication's purpose?

A. "This medication will help lower my blood pressure and reduce the risk of complications."

B. "Taking this medication will prevent me from developing gestational diabetes."

C. "The medication will provide pain relief after my cesarean section surgery."

Q28: A postpartum woman who is prescribed diuretics asks the nurse about the potential side effects. Which response by the nurse is appropriate?

A. "Diuretics may cause increased urination and electrolyte imbalances."

B. "Diuretics can lead to drowsiness and dizziness."

C. "Diuretics may result in gastrointestinal upset and constipation."

Q29: A postpartum woman presents with symptoms of painful, swollen veins in the rectal area. The nurse suspects the woman may be experiencing hemorrhoids. What nursing intervention is appropriate for managing hemorrhoids in the postpartum period?

A. Encouraging the woman to sit on a soft cushion or inflatable donut-shaped pillow

B. Applying warm compresses to the affected area after each bowel movement

C. Assisting with the administration of stool softeners as prescribed

Q30: A postpartum woman complains of lower abdominal pain and discomfort due to bladder distention and urinary retention. What nursing intervention is appropriate for managing bladder distention and urinary retention in the postpartum period?

A. Assisting the woman to a comfortable position and encouraging frequent voiding

B. Performing gentle fundal massage to promote bladder emptying

C. Providing analgesics to relieve pain and discomfort

Q31: A postpartum woman complains of persistent lower abdominal pain and difficulty urinating. On assessment, the nurse palpates a distended bladder above the symphysis pubis. What complication is the woman most likely experiencing?

A. Bladder distention and urinary retention

B. Hemorrhoids

C. Afterpains

Q32: A postpartum woman asks the nurse about the importance of postpartum self-care. Which statement by the woman indicates a need for further education?

A. "I should take time for rest and sleep when the baby is sleeping."

B. "I need to avoid lifting heavy objects for at least six weeks."

C. "I should resume my pre-pregnancy exercise routine immediately."

Q33: A postpartum woman expresses her concerns about choosing an appropriate contraception method. Which statement by the woman indicates an understanding of effective contraception?

A. "I'm planning to exclusively breastfeed, so I won't need any contraception."

B. "I'm considering using an intrauterine device IUD for long-term contraception."

C. "I'll rely on the calendar method to track my menstrual cycle and avoid pregnancy."

Q34: A nursing mother asks about the composition of breast milk. Which statement accurately describes the components of breast milk?

A. "Breast milk contains carbohydrates proteins and fats providing essential nutrients for the baby's growth and development."

B. "Breast milk is composed mainly of water, with small amounts of electrolytes and vitamins."

C. "Breast milk consists primarily of antibodies and immune cells, offering protection against infections."

Q35: A nursing mother asks about the anatomy or physiology of lactation. Which statement accurately describes the process of lactation?

A. Breastfeeding is an intricate process where the mammary glands synthesize or secrete breast milk in response to hormonal signals.

B. "Lactation is primarily controlled by the baby's suckling and the stimulation of nerve endings in the nipples, leading to milk production."

C. "Lactation is a passive process where breast milk is automatically produced and stored in the mammary glands for feeding."

Q36: A nurse is providing breastfeeding education to a group of new mothers. One mother asks about the frequency and duration of breastfeeding sessions. What information should the nurse provide?

A. "Newborns typically breastfeed every 2 to 3 hours, with each session lasting approximately 10 to 15 minutes per breast."

B. "Newborns should breastfeed on demand, as often as they show hunger cues, with each session lasting as long as the baby needs."

C. "Newborns should breastfeed every 4 to 5 hours, with each session lasting no more than 5 minutes per breast."

Q37: A nurse is providing education on the normal breastfeeding process to a group of new mothers. Which factor is essential for successful breastfeeding and optimal milk transfer?

A. Positioning

B. Latch On

C. Suck/Swallow Sequence

Q38: A lactating mother is experiencing breast engorgement and seeks advice on relieving discomfort through hand expression. The nurse explains the key points of normal hand expression. Which key point is crucial for ensuring effective milk removal?

A. Positioning

B. Latch On

C. Timing (Frequency and Duration)

Q39: A lactating mother is planning to return to work and wants to continue providing breast milk to her baby. Which key point of breast care should the nurse emphasize when discussing expressing and storing breast milk?

A. Use of Supplementary Feedings

B. Use of Breastfeeding Devices

C. Expressing and Storing Breast Milk

Q40: A postpartum woman is concerned about low milk supply and wants to increase her milk production. Which key point of breast care should the nurse focus on when providing education and support to the mother?

A. Use of Supplementary Feedings

B. Use of Breastfeeding Devices

C. Expressing and Storing Breast Milk

Q41: A lactating woman wants to build up a supply of stored breast milk for future use. Which key point of nipple care should be emphasized to maintain milk supply and prevent engorgement?

A. Regularly massaging the breasts to stimulate milk production

B. Applying warm compresses before each breastfeeding session

C. Using a breast pump to express milk between feedings

Q42: A postpartum woman has been diagnosed with a severe case of breast engorgement which is causing significant discomfort and pain. In this case what factor would make breastfeeding not recommended?

A. Maternal complications

B. Latch-on problems

C. Breast engorgement

Q43: A pregnant woman with a history of perinatal substance abuse is seeking advice on breastfeeding her newborn What could prevent breastfeeding in this situation?

A. Insufficient milk supply

B. Therapeutic medications

C. Maternal illness

Q44: A breastfeeding mother requires hospitalization for a surgical procedure. The nurse educates the mother about maintaining lactation during her separation from the newborn. The recommended approach for sustaining lactation is to:

A. Regularly express breast milk using a breast pump

B. Initiate bottle feeding with formula to prevent milk production

C. Temporarily stop breastfeeding until the mother is reunited with the newborn

Q45: A breastfeeding mother is concerned about her newborn's jaundice. The nurse explains that breastfeeding can help prevent hyperbilirubinemia by:

A. Promoting adequate hydration

B. Facilitating weight loss in the newborn

C. Enhancing newborn's immune system

Q46: A term newborn is born to a mother with gestational diabetes. The nurse closely monitors the baby for signs of hypoglycemia due to:

A. Excessive insulin production by the newborn's pancreas

B. Insufficient insulin production by the newborn's pancreas

C. Maternal hyperglycemia during pregnancy

Q47: A couple who recently became parents is experiencing changes in their marital relationship. Which statement best reflects a normal characteristic of the parental relationship during the postpartum period?

A. Feeling a deep sense of satisfaction and fulfillment in their relationship

B. Experiencing increased conflicts and disagreements over parenting decisions

C. Displaying a complete loss of interest in their relationship due to the baby's arrival

Q48: A nurse is providing discharge teaching to a postpartum woman who experienced a cesarean birth. The nurse discusses the importance of proper incision care to prevent infection. Which statement made by the woman indicates a need for further teaching?

A. "I should wash the incision site gently with mild soap and water."

B. "I will monitor the incision site for any signs of redness, swelling, or drainage."

C. "It's important to change the dressing over the incision every day."

Q49: A postpartum nurse is caring for a woman who is experiencing postpartum blues. The nurse understands that postpartum blues are characterized by which of the following?

A. Intense and persistent feelings of sadness and hopelessness

B. Onset within the first week after childbirth and resolves within two weeks

C. Symptoms that significantly impair the woman's ability to function

Q50: A postpartum nurse is providing education to a woman who is concerned about breastfeeding her newborn due to her older child's aggressive behavior. The nurse recognizes that the older child's aggression may be a result of adjustment difficulties. Which statement by the nurse would be most appropriate in this situation?

A. "It's best to wean your newborn from breastfeeding to prevent the older child from feeling left out."

B. "You should scold and punish your older child whenever they display aggressive behavior towards the newborn."

C. "Try to involve your older child in breastfeeding sessions by allowing them to bring you items or read books nearby."

Q51: A postpartum nurse is providing education to a woman who is concerned about the impact of her return to work on her ability to bond with her newborn. Which statement by the nurse provides accurate information regarding work-related barriers to parent/infant interactions?

A. "Returning to work can enhance the bonding process between the parent and the infant."

B. "Infants of working mothers have a higher risk of attachment disorders."

C. "Maintaining regular, quality time with your baby outside of work hours can help strengthen the parent/infant bond."

Q52: A postpartum nurse is providing education on the impact of cultural practices and beliefs on family integration. The nurse explains that cultural practices can both facilitate and hinder family integration. Which example demonstrates a cultural practice that may hinder family integration?

A. Extended family members actively participate in caring for and supporting the new parents.

B. Gender roles and expectations restrict the involvement of fathers in infant care.

C. Cultural celebrations and rituals promote family togetherness and bonding.

Q53: A postpartum nurse is caring for a family with a newborn and identifies a potential cultural barrier to family integration. The family belongs to a culture that places high value on gender roles and expectations. Which intervention would be most appropriate for the nurse to support family integration in this context?

A. Educating the family about the benefits of challenging traditional gender roles and expectations.

B. Encouraging open communication and negotiation of gender roles within the family.

C. Discouraging the family from questioning or challenging their cultural beliefs and practices.

Q54: A postpartum nurse is providing support to a woman who has disclosed intimate partner violence. The nurse is assisting the woman in developing a safety plan. Which action would be a priority in the safety plan?

A. Encouraging the woman to confront her partner about the abuse.

B. Identifying a safe place for the woman or her children to go in an emergency.

C. Advising the woman to minimize contact with family and friends for their safety.

Q55: During a postpartum assessment, a nurse observes signs of intimate partner violence (IPV) in a new mother. Which action should the nurse prioritize to ensure the safety and wellbeing of both the mother and the newborn?

A. Documenting the observations and reporting the findings to the appropriate healthcare professionals.

B. Confronting the mother about the suspected IPV and encouraging her to seek help immediately.

C. Contacting child protective services to initiate an investigation into the family's situation.

Q56: During a postpartum visit a birth mother who has chosen adoption for her baby expresses feelings of grief and loss. Which action by the nurse demonstrates appropriate psychosocial support in this situation?

A. Validating the mother's feelings and providing empathy and understanding.

B. Encouraging the mother to focus on her decision as a positive and move forward.

C. Suggesting that the mother seek counseling to overcome her feelings of grief.

Q57: A nurse is caring for a woman who recently gave birth to a baby with a life-limiting condition. What is the most important aspect of care for this woman and her family during this difficult time?

A. Providing emotional support and creating opportunities for the family to create lasting memories with their baby.

B. Encouraging the family to avoid discussing the baby's condition to prevent additional emotional distress.

C. Focusing solely on the medical aspects and treatment options for the baby's condition.

Q58: A postpartum woman requests not to be informed about her newborn's genetic test results, as she is worried about the potential implications. Which ethical principle should the healthcare provider consider when deciding how to approach this situation?

A. Autonomy

B. Beneficence

C. Nonmaleficence

Q59: A nurse is assessing a newborn's hips and observes limited hip abduction with a palpable click or clunk. What condition should the nurse suspect?

A. Developmental dysplasia of the hip

B. Talipes equinovarus (clubfoot)

C. Cleft lip and palate

Q60: A newborn presents with facial asymmetry, a tilted head, and limited neck movement. What condition should the nurse suspect?

A. Torticollis

B. Craniosynostosis

C. Cleft lip and palate

Q61: A nurse is assessing a newborn's temperature using a temporal artery thermometer. Which site should the nurse choose for accurate temperature measurement?

A. Forehead

B. Neck

C. Axilla

Q62: A newborn is suspected to have hemolytic disease of the newborn (HDN). Which laboratory test is essential to confirm the diagnosis?

A. Direct Coombs test

B. Indirect Coombs test

C. Blood culture

Q63: A nurse is monitoring a newborn's bilirubin levels. Which laboratory value would be considered within the normal range for a term newborn?

A. Total serum bilirubin level of 10 mg/dL

B. Total serum bilirubin level of 15 mg/dL

C. Total serum bilirubin level of 20 mg/dL

Q64: A nurse is assessing a newborn's physical characteristics to determine gestational age. Which finding is consistent with a late preterm newborn?

A. Abundant lanugo over the entire body

B. Minimal flexion of the extremities

C. Scanty vernix caseosa

Q65: A newborn is born at term. Which physical characteristic would be expected in a term newborn?

A. Fused eyelids

B. Abundant plantar creases

C. Minimal breast tissue development

Q66: A nurse is performing a neurobehavioral assessment on a newborn and observes the presence of the stepping reflex. What does this reflex indicate?

A. Ability to coordinate voluntary movements

B. Sensory integration of the lower extremities

C. Development of fine motor skills

Q67: A newborn exhibits a strong suck reflex during a sensory assessment. What is the purpose of this reflex?

A. To facilitate feeding and swallowing

B. To enhance visual tracking abilities

C. To promote postural stability

Q68: A preeclamptic woman in the immediate postpartum period needs to be monitored closely for elevated blood pressure and:

A. Adult respiratory distress syndrome

B. Onset of seizures

C. Subdural hematoma

Q69: During a newborn's assessment, the nurse observes oozing and foul odor around the umbilical cord stump. What action should the nurse take in this situation?

A. Cleanse the area with hydrogen peroxide and apply a sterile dressing.

B. Notify the healthcare provider immediately.

C. Cleanse the area with warm water or mild soap and monitor for signs of infection.

Q70: A nurse is providing education to new parents about promoting healthy elimination patterns in their newborn. Which recommendation should the nurse include?

A. Encourage the newborn to drink plenty of water to prevent dehydration.

B. Perform gentle abdominal massage to stimulate bowel movements.

C. Use petroleum jelly on the perineal area to prevent diaper rash.

Q71: A parent asks the nurse about the potential complications of circumcision. Which complication should the nurse mention?

A. Having a higher chance of urinary tract infections.

B. Excessive bleeding at the circumcision site.

C. Delayed bonding between the parent and newborn.

Q72: A parent asks the nurse about techniques to relieve gas and colic in their newborn. Which suggestion should the nurse provide?

A. Burp the newborn frequently during feedings and try gentle tummy massage.

B. Avoid breastfeeding or bottle-feeding for longer durations to prevent overfeeding.

C. Offer the newborn a pacifier dipped in sugar water to soothe colic.

Q73: A newborn is experiencing diaper rash. Which comfort measure should the nurse recommend to alleviate the discomfort?

A. Frequent diaper changes and gentle cleansing with warm water

B. Applying talcum powder to the affected area after each diaper change

C. Using scented wipes to keep the diaper area fresh and clean

Q74: A nurse is explaining the purpose of the car seat challenge test to parents. What information should the nurse provide?

A. The car seat challenge test assesses the newborn's ability to maintain oxygen levels and breathing while in a car seat.

B. The car seat challenge test measures the newborn's tolerance to different car seat positions.

C. The car seat challenge test evaluates the newborn's ability to self-soothe and fall asleep in a car seat.

Q75: A parent asks the nurse about the importance of rear-facing car seats for newborns. What should the nurse explain?

A. Rear facing car seats provide better support and protection for the newborn's head neck and spine.

B. Rear facing car seats allow the newborn to see the surroundings more easily.

C. Rear-facing car seats are less expensive compared to forward-facing car seats.

Q76: A newborn has dry, flaky skin. What should the nurse recommend to promote skin hydration?

A. Applying a fragrance-free, hypoallergenic moisturizing cream to the newborn's skin

B. Increasing the frequency of bathing to moisturize the skin

C. Exposing the newborn's skin to direct sunlight for short periods

Q77: A parent asks the nurse about preventing diaper rash in their newborn. What is the nurse's best response?

A. "Change the newborn's diaper frequently and apply a zinc oxide-based diaper cream."

B. "Use scented baby wipes to clean the diaper area for added freshness."

C. "Avoid using any diaper cream or ointment to allow the skin to breathe."

Q78: A nurse is providing education to parents about safe sleep practices. What should the nurse include as a risk factor for sudden infant death syndrome SIDS?

A. Co-sleeping with parents

B. Placing the newborn on their side to sleep

C. Using a pacifier during sleep

Q79: A parent asks the nurse about safe sleep guidelines for their newborn when visiting friends or family. What is the nurse's best response?

A. "Ensure that a safe sleep environment is available for your newborn such as a crib or bassinet."

B. "It is acceptable to let your newborn sleep in a car seat or on a couch during visits."

C. "Allowing your newborn to sleep in a bed with others is safe and promotes bonding."

Q80: A nurse is providing education to parents about the use of analgesics in newborns. When are analgesics typically administered to newborns?

A. Before and during a painful procedure or surgery

B. As a routine medication to promote comfort and relaxation

C. After the newborn show's signs of pain or discomfort

Q81: A newborn is receiving a vaccination. Why do we give vaccines to newborns?

A. To stimulate the immune system and provide long lasting protection against specific diseases

B. To promote growth and development in the newborn

C. To prevent common cold and respiratory infections in the newborn

Q82: A newborn is born with central cyanosis, decreased muscle tone, and a heart rate of 80 beats per minute. What could be the most likely reason for these findings in your opinion?

A. Hypovolemia

B. Hypothermia

C. Hypoglycemia

Q83: A newborn is born with poor respiratory effort and a heart rate of 50 beats per minute. The newborn is receiving positive pressure ventilation without improvement. What is the next step in the management of this newborn?

A. Administer epinephrine intravenously

B. Initiate chest compressions

C. Perform endotracheal intubation

Q84: When performing chest compressions during newborn resuscitation, what is the recommended compression-to-ventilation ratio?

A. 3:1

B. 5:1

C. 15:2

Q85: After initiating chest compressions, when should reassessment of heart rate be performed during newborn resuscitation?

A. After 30 seconds of chest compressions

B. After 1 minute of chest compressions

C. After 2 minutes of chest compressions

Q86: In the prevention of neonatal hypoglycemia, what medication may be administered to newborns at risk?

A. Glucose gel

B. Dopamine

C. Sodium bicarbonate

Q87: What medication is typically administered to newborns born to mothers with positive hepatitis B surface antigen Hesitates?

A. Hepatitis B immunoglobulin (HBIG)

B. Measles-mumps-rubella (MMR) vaccine

C. Varicella vaccine

Q88: A newborn with respiratory distress was administered exogenous surfactant. What finding suggests that the intervention is effective?

A. Persistent tachypnea

B. Increased oxygen requirement

C. Improved lung compliance

Q89: A newborn with suspected congenital heart disease received prostaglandin E1 (PGE1). Which finding indicates the effectiveness of the intervention?

A. Worsening cyanosis

B. Decreased heart rate

C. Increased murmur intensity

Q90: A newborn scores 8 on the Apgar scale at 5 minutes after birth. What does this score indicate?

A. The newborn is in excellent condition.

B. The newborn is in good condition but requires ongoing observation.

C. The score is low, and the newborn needs immediate medical intervention.

Q91: Which Apgar score reflects a newborn's poor muscle tone, weak respiratory effort, and no response to stimulation?

A. 0

B. 4

C. 7

Q92: When caring for a woman with postpartum hemorrhage, the nurse should prioritize which of the following interventions?

A. Administering IV fluids

B. Assessing vital signs

C. Massaging the uterus

Q93: The primary assessment finding in a woman with postpartum hemorrhage is:

A. Tachycardia

B. Hypotension

C. Pale skin color

Q94: Treatment for postpartum thrombophlebitis may include:

A. Anticoagulant medication

B. Antibiotic therapy

C. Surgical intervention

Q95: The nurse should assess for which of the following complications associated with postpartum thrombophlebitis?

A. Pulmonary embolism

B. Urinary tract infection

C. Postpartum depression

Q96: The most common sign of a pulmonary embolism is:

A. Chest pain

B. Shortness of breath

C. Palpitations

Q97: The diagnostic test of choice for confirming the presence of pulmonary embolus is:

A. Chest x-ray

B. Electrocardiogram (ECG)

C. Computed tomography angiography CTA

Q98: Treatment for pulmonary embolus may include:

A. Anticoagulant therapy

B. Antibiotic administration

C. Surgical removal of blood clots

Q99: Laboratory findings consistent with DIC include:

A. Prolonged prothrombin time (PT) and activated partial thromboplastin time (apt)

B. Decreased platelet count

C. Elevated red blood cell count

Q100: The treatment of DIC focuses on:

A. Treating the underlying cause and providing supportive care

B. Administering antibiotics to control infection

C. Performing surgical interventions to remove blood clots

Q101: The management of HELLP syndrome involves:

A. Prompt delivery of the fetus and supportive care

B. Administration of anticoagulant medications

C. Continuous fetal monitoring and bed rest

Q102: Nursing interventions for a woman with HELLP syndrome include:

A. Monitoring blood pressure and urine output

B. Encouraging increased fluid intake

C. Administering diuretic medications

Q103: Complications associated with a perineal hematoma include:

A. Infection

B. Delayed wound healing

C. Urinary retention

Q104: The assessment findings of a perineal hematoma may reveal:

A. Ecchymosis and tenderness

B. Elevated white blood cell count

C. Decreased urine output

Q105: The nursing intervention to promote comfort in a woman with a perineal hematoma includes:

A. Administering analgesics as prescribed

B. Encouraging ambulation and frequent position changes

C. Applying warm compresses to the affected area

Q106: Chronic hypertension increases the risk of developing:

A. Preterm premature rupture of membranes (PPROM)

B. Gestational trophoblastic disease

C. Preeclampsia

Q107: Monitoring blood pressure is essential during pregnancy for women with chronic hypertension. What is the recommended frequency for blood pressure checks?

A. Every 4 weeks

B. Every 8 weeks

C. Every 12 weeks

Q108: Chronic hypertension increases the risk of developing which neonatal complication?

A. Neonatal hypoglycemia

B. Respiratory distress syndrome

C. Hyperbilirubinemia

Q109: Gestational hypertension differs from chronic hypertension in that it:

A. Persists beyond 12 weeks postpartum

B. Resolves within 12 weeks postpartum

C. Requires continuous monitoring during labor

Q110: Maternal complications associated with gestational hypertension include:

A. Placental abruption

B. Cardiac arrhythmias

C. Pulmonary embolism

Q111: The mainstay of treatment for eclampsia is:

A. Magnesium sulfate

B. Oxytocin

C. Antibiotics

Q112: Maternal complications associated with eclampsia include:

A. Pulmonary edema

B. Renal failure

C. Thyroid storm

Q113: The recommended treatment for endometritis is:

A. Intravenous antibiotics

B. Topical antifungal cream

C. Nonsteroidal anti-inflammatory drugs NSAIDs

A. Lower abdominal pain

B. Breast engorgement

C. Decreased urinary frequency

Q115: Complications of a severe or untreated wound infection may include:

A. Abscess formation

B. Postpartum hemorrhage

C. Thromboembolism

Q116: The most important nursing intervention for a woman with a wound infection is:

A. Proper wound care and hygiene

B. Encouraging ambulation

C. Providing emotional support

Q117: Postpartum education should include instructions on signs of a wound infection, such as:

A. Increased pain and swelling at the incision site

B. Breast engorgement

C. Increased urinary frequency

Q118: Complications of septic pelvic thrombophlebitis may include:

A. Pulmonary embolism

B. Sepsis

C. Endometritis

Q119: The most important nursing intervention for a woman with septic pelvic thrombophlebitis is:

A. Administering prescribed antibiotics

B. Monitoring vital signs and symptoms

C. Providing emotional support

Q120: Postpartum education should include instructions on signs of worsening septic pelvic thrombophlebitis, such as:

A. Increasing pelvic pain and tenderness

B. Breast engorgement

C. Decreased urinary output

Q121: Complications of untreated postpartum UTIs may include:

A. Pyelonephritis (kidney infection)

B. Endometritis

C. Thrombophlebitis

Q122: The best preventive measure for postpartum UTIs is:

A. Adequate perineal hygiene

B. Voiding regularly

C. Prophylactic antibiotic use

Q123: Postpartum education should include instructions on signs of worsening UTI, such as:

A. Increased urinary urgency

B. Flank pain

C. Breast engorgement

Q124: Women with gestational diabetes are advised to monitor their blood glucose levels regularly. What is the target fasting blood glucose level for these women?

A. Less than 90 mg/dL

B. Less than 110 mg/dL

C. Less than 130 mg/dL

Q125: Women with gestational diabetes are often managed through diet and exercise modifications. If blood glucose levels remain uncontrolled, what is the next step in management?

A. Insulin therapy

B. Oral antidiabetic medications

C. Continuous glucose monitoring

Q126: Which of the following relaxation techniques may help postpartum women with sleep difficulties?

A. Listening to loud music

B. Taking a warm bath before bed

C. Engaging in vigorous exercise

Q127: What is the role of a supportive partner in assisting a postpartum woman with sleep disturbances?

A. Ensuring the baby's needs are met during the night

B. Taking over night-time feeding responsibilities

C. Offering emotional support and reassurance

Q128: Postpartum women with sleep disturbances should be educated about the importance of self-care. Which self-care practice may improve sleep quality?

A. Engaging in excessive physical activity

B. Limiting fluid intake before bed

C. Consuming high amounts of caffeine

Q129 Among these factors, which one is linked to a higher chance of developing postpartum depression?

A. High socioeconomic status

B. Lack of social support

C. Multiparity

Q130: In addressing postpartum depression, the primary treatment typically involves a mix of psychotherapy and pharmacotherapy. For this condition, which class of antidepressant medications is commonly recommended by healthcare professionals?

A. Selective serotonin reuptake inhibitors SSRI

B. Benzodiazepines

C. Tricyclic antidepressants TCA

Q131 Postpartum depression can have an impact on the mother's capability to care for her newborn baby. What is an important nursing intervention to support maternal-infant bonding in the presence of postpartum depression?

A. Encouraging the mother to rely solely on her support network

B. Providing education on infant care and development

C. Recommending separation between the mother and infant

Q132: Neonates born to mothers who use substances during pregnancy may exhibit withdrawal symptoms. Which of the following is a characteristic sign of neonatal withdrawal?

A. Decreased muscle tone

B. Excessive sleepiness

C. High-pitched crying

Q133: Screening for substance abuse during pregnancy is important to identify women who may need additional support and interventions. Which of the following screening tools is commonly used for this purpose?

A. Alcohol Use Disorders Identification Test (AUDIT)

B. Drug Abuse Screening Test (DAST)

C. CAGE questionnaire

Q134: Newborns with cyanotic heart disease may experience episodes of acute cyanosis and respiratory distress known as "Tet spells." What is the appropriate nursing intervention for a newborn experiencing a Tet spell?

A. Place the newborn in a knee-to-chest position

B. Administer supplemental oxygen via nasal cannula

C. Encourage the newborn to cry vigorously

Q135: Tetralogy of Fallot is a type of cyanotic heart disease. Which of the following anatomical abnormalities is associated with Tetralogy of Fallot?

A. Pulmonary stenosis

B. Atrial septal defect (ASD)

C. Coarctation of the aorta

Q136: Newborns with cyanotic heart disease may experience episodes of cyanosis and hypoxia. What nursing intervention should be prioritized during a cyanotic episode?

A. Administer supplemental oxygen

B. Administer a diuretic medication

C. Initiate cardiopulmonary resuscitation CPR

Q137: A nurse is caring for a newborn with a cyanotic heart disease As we create the nursing care plan for this infant, which of these interventions should we make sure to include?

A. Administering medications to decrease pulmonary artery pressure.

B. Monitoring for signs of cyanosis and respiratory distress.

C. Providing oxygen supplementation to improve oxygenation.

Q138: A newborn is diagnosed with central apnea. Which of the following statements accurately describes central apnea?

A. Central apnea happens when the airway is blocked, interrupting breathing.

B. Central apnea is characterized by a lack of respiratory effort due to immaturity of the respiratory centers in the brain.

C. Central apnea is a result of muscle weakness and inability to maintain normal breathing.

Q139: A newborn is diagnosed with Transient Tachypnea of the Newborn (TTN). Which of the following interventions is typically indicated for infants with TTN?

A. Administration of antibiotics to treat potential infections.

B. Supplemental oxygen therapy to improve oxygenation.

C. Initiation of cardiopulmonary resuscitation CPR for respiratory distress.

Q140: A newborn is diagnosed with pneumothorax. Which of the following interventions is typically indicated for infants with pneumothorax?

A. Administration of antibiotics to treat potential infections.

B. Placement of a chest tube to evacuate the accumulated air.

C. Initiation of cardiopulmonary resuscitation CPR for respiratory distress.

Q141: A newborn is diagnosed with meconium aspiration syndrome. Which of the following interventions is typically indicated for infants with this condition?

A. Administration of antibiotics to treat potential infections.

B. Suctioning of the airways to remove meconium and clear the lungs.

C. Initiation of oxygen therapy to improve oxygenation.

Q142: A newborn is diagnosed with seizures. Which of the following interventions is typically indicated for infants experiencing seizures?

A. Administration of pain medication to relieve discomfort.

B. Immediate referral to a developmental specialist.

C. Prompt medical evaluation and initiation of anti-seizure medications.

Q143: A newborn is diagnosed with jitteriness. Which of the following interventions is typically indicated for a newborn experiencing jitteriness?

A. Administration of pain medication to relieve discomfort.

B. Immediate referral to a developmental specialist.

C. Evaluation of blood glucose levels and appropriate management.

Q144: A newborn is diagnosed with intracranial hemorrhage. For a newborn with intracranial hemorrhage, which of these interventions is usually recommended?

A. Observation without any specific treatment.

B. Administration of pain medication to alleviate discomfort.

C. Referral to a specialist for surgical intervention or medical management.

Q145: A pregnant woman asks about the risk factors for neural tube defects. Which of the following statements accurately describes maternal risk factors for neural tube defects?

A. "Advanced maternal age is a protective factor against neural tube defects."

B. "Maternal obesity is not associated with an increased risk of neural tube defects."

C. When the mother has diabetes or takes specific antiepileptic medications it can raise the likelihood of neural tube defects.

Q146: A nurse is providing education to a group of pregnant women regarding the effects of substance abuse on the developing fetus. Which of the following statements accurately describes the neurological consequences of substance abuse during pregnancy?

A. "Substance abuse during pregnancy has no impact on the neurological development of the fetus."

B. " "When a pregnant woman abuses substances, it can lead to lasting cognitive and behavioral problems in the child.

C. "Neurological consequences of substance abuse are limited to temporary withdrawal symptoms after birth."

Q147: A nurse is providing education to parents about intussusception in infants. Which of the following statements accurately describes intussusception?

A. It is a telescoping of one segment of the intestine into an adjacent segment, causing obstruction.

B. It is a congenital malformation where the intestines protrude through a defect in the abdominal wall.

C. It is a condition where the intestines twist upon themselves, causing obstruction and compromised blood supply.

Q148: A nurse is caring for a newborn with gastroschisis. Which of the following statements accurately describes this condition?

A. It is a protrusion of abdominal contents through a defect in the abdominal wall near the umbilicus.

B. It is an abnormal opening in the diaphragm, allowing abdominal organs to herniate into the chest cavity.

C. It is a failure of the intestines to return to the abdominal cavity during fetal development.

Q149: A newborn is diagnosed with polycythemia. Which intervention should the nurse prioritize for this newborn?

A. Administering partial exchange transfusion

B. Encouraging frequent breastfeeding sessions

C. Providing oxygen supplementation

Q150: A newborn is diagnosed with vitamin K deficiency. Which clotting factor is primarily affected by this deficiency?

A. Factor II (Prothrombin)

B. Factor V (Proaccelerin)

C. Factor VIII (Antihemophilic factor)

Q151: Which route of administration is commonly used to provide vitamin K supplementation to newborns?

A. Intramuscular injection

B. Oral administration

C. Intravenous infusion

Q152: A newborn with hyperbilirubinemia is prescribed phototherapy. Which action by the nurse is essential during phototherapy?

A. Monitoring the newborn's temperature

B. Administering vitamin K supplementation

C. Encouraging breastfeeding every 2 hours

Q153: A newborn is diagnosed with ABO incompatibility. Among the following blood types which one is most susceptible to significant hyperbilirubinemia?

A. O positive

B. A positive

C. AB positive

Q154: In ABO incompatibility, which antibody is present in the maternal serum and is responsible for hemolysis of the newborn's red blood cells?

A. Anti-A antibody

B. Anti-B antibody

C. Anti-D antibody

Q155: What is the primary concern in the management of a newborn with hemolytic disease?

A. Ways to prevent hyperbilirubinemia.

B. Prevention of respiratory distress

C. Prevention of anemia

Q156: Which of the following medications should be avoided in individuals with G6PD deficiency due to the risk of hemolysis?

A. Penicillin

B. Ibuprofen

C. Acetaminophen

Q157: What is the inheritance pattern of G6PD deficiency?

A. Autosomal recessive

B. Autosomal dominant

C. X-linked recessive

Q158: A newborn with polycythemia is at increased risk for which complication related to blood viscosity?

A. Hemorrhage

B. Thrombosis

C. Infection

Q159: The nurse is providing discharge teaching to the parents of a neonate with polycythemia. Which instruction should the nurse include to prevent future episodes?

A. Encourage frequent breastfeeding or formula feeding.

B. Avoid exposure to extreme temperatures.

C. Administer anticoagulant medications as prescribed.

Q160: When assessing a newborn for hyper viscosity, the nurse should prioritize which diagnostic test?

A. Blood viscosity measurement

B. Complete blood count (CBC)

C. Blood coagulation studies

Q161: When assessing a newborn for thrombocytopenia, the nurse should prioritize which diagnostic test?

A. Platelet count

B. Complete blood count (CBC)

C. Coagulation profile

Q162: When assessing a newborn for neonatal sepsis, the nurse should prioritize which diagnostic test?

A. Blood culture

B. Complete blood count (CBC)

C. Lumbar puncture

Q163: The nurse is caring for a newborn with suspected sepsis. Which of the following lab results would be most indicative of an infection?

A. Decreased neutrophil count

B. Decreased lymphocyte count

C. Increased monocyte count

Q164: In addition to the CBC, which additional laboratory test is commonly ordered to help identify the causative agent of an infection in a newborn?

A. Blood culture

B. Stool culture

C. Urine culture

Q165: A newborn is scheduled for a lumbar puncture. What action should the nurse take prior to the procedure?

A. Administer a sedative to the newborn

B. Obtain informed consent from the parents

C. Withhold feeding for 24 hours

Q166: When explaining the lumbar puncture procedure to the parents of a newborn, which information should the nurse include?

A. The procedure involves inserting a needle into the spinal cord

B. The newborn will receive general anesthesia during the procedure

C. The newborn may experience some discomfort during the procedure

Q167: A newborn is diagnosed with congenital rubella syndrome. What are the typical signs or findings commonly linked to this condition?

A. Micrognathia (small jaw)

B. Webbed neck

C. Clubfoot

Q168: A pregnant woman is diagnosed with gonorrhea. What is the recommended action to prevent passing gonorrhea to the newborn during childbirth?

A. Administering prophylactic antibiotics to the newborn

B. Offering guidance and encouragement to the woman, advocating for a vaginal birth over a cesarean section.

C. Applying silver nitrate solution to the newborn's eyes

Q169: A newborn is suspected to have congenital human immunodeficiency virus HIV infection. What is the appropriate nursing action regarding feeding for this newborn?

A. Encouraging exclusive breastfeeding to enhance the newborn's immunity

B. Providing formula feeding instead of breastfeeding to reduce the risk of transmission

C. Administering antiretroviral therapy to the newborn before breastfeeding

Q170 The medical team identifies that the newborn has an infection caused by methicillin-resistant Staphylococcus aureus MRSA.

A. Ceftriaxone

B. Vancomycin

C. Ampicillin-sulbactam

Q171: After diagnosing a urinary tract infection caused by Escherichia coli in a pregnant woman, what is the usual antibiotic prescribed for treating E. coli infections during pregnancy?

A. Penicillin G

B. Ciprofloxacin

C. Nitrofurantoin

Q172: The most common cause of hypoglycemia in newborns is:

A. Maternal diabetes

B. Prematurity

C. Inadequate caloric intake

Q173: Inborn errors of metabolism are typically inherited in which pattern?

A. Autosomal dominant

B. Autosomal recessive

C. X-linked recessive

Q173: A pregnant woman is found to have an X-linked recessive disorder. What is the probability that her male fetus will inherit the disorder?

A. 0%

B. 25%

C. 50%

Q175: An infant of a diabetic mother is at increased risk for which of the following complications?

A. Respiratory distress syndrome RDS

B. Hyperbilirubinemia

C. Hypothermia

Test 3 Answer Key

1	B	27	A	53	B
2	A	28	A	54	B
3	C	29	A	55	A
4	A	30	A	56	A
5	B	31	A	57	A
6	A	32	C	58	A
7	B	33	B	59	A
8	C	34	A	60	A
9	C	35	A	61	A
10	C	36	B	62	B
11	B	37	B	63	A
12	B	38	C	64	C
13	B	39	C	65	B
14	C	40	A	66	B
15	A	41	C	67	A
16	C	42	C	68	B
17	C	43	C	69	C
18	A	44	A	70	B
19	A	45	A	71	B
20	B	46	C	72	A
21	B	47	B	73	A
22	A	48	C	74	A
23	C	49	B	75	A
24	C	50	C	76	A
25	C	51	C	77	A
26	B	52	B	78	A

79	A	106	C	133	B
80	A	107	A	134	A
81	A	108	B	135	A
82	B	109	B	136	A
83	A	110	A	137	B
84	C	111	A	138	B
85	B	112	B	139	B
86	A	113	A	140	B
87	A	114	A	141	B
88	C	115	A	142	C
89	B	116	A	143	C
90	B	117	A	144	C
91	A	118	A	145	C
92	C	119	B	146	B
93	A	120	A	147	A
94	A	121	A	148	A
95	A	122	A	149	A
96	B	123	B	150	A
97	C	124	A	151	A
98	A	125	A	152	A
99	A	126	B	153	C
100	A	127	C	154	B
101	A	128	B	155	A
102	A	129	B	156	B
103	B	130	A	157	C
104	A	131	B	158	B
105	A	132	C	159	B

160	C	166	C	172	B
161	A	167	A	173	B
162	A	168	A	174	C
163	A	169	B	175	B
164	A	170	B		
165	B	171	C		

Maternal Newborn Nursing Exam Practice Test 4
Pregnancy, Birth Risk Factors, and Complications

Q1: Which antenatal factor is associated with an increased risk of placenta previa during pregnancy?

A. Advanced maternal age

B. Previous cesarean section

C. Nulliparity

Q2: Advanced maternal age is considered a risk factor for which of the following conditions during pregnancy?

A. Gestational diabetes

B. Preterm labor

C. All of the above

Q3 During pregnancy ensuring proper nutrition is vital to support the wellbeing and growth of both the mother and the baby. Folic acid is a significant nutrient that pregnant women should focus on. Which statement about folic acid supplementation during pregnancy is accurate?

A. Folic acid supplementation is necessary to prevent neural tube defects in the baby.

B For pregnant women taking folic acid supplements is typically advised but it's particularly recommended for those with a family history of neural tube defects.

C. Folic acid supplementation is not necessary if the woman consumes a diet rich in folate-rich foods

Q4: Obstetrical history is an important factor in assessing pregnancy and birth risk factors. Among the following obstetrical histories, which one is linked to a higher likelihood of placenta previa?

A. Previous cesarean birth

B. Nulliparity (no previous pregnancies)

C. Maternal age over 35 years

Q5: A pregnant woman from a cultural background that values family support and collective decision-making expresses her desire to have her mother present during labor and childbirth. Which action by the nurse demonstrates culturally sensitive care?

A. Explaining to the woman that only one support person is allowed in the delivery room

B. Encouraging the woman to reconsider her decision and rely solely on her partner for support

C. Collaborating with the healthcare team to accommodate the woman's request for her mother's presence

Q6: What is a recognized risk factor for female infertility among the following options?

A. Advanced maternal age

B. Male partner's smoking habit

C. High caffeine consumption

Q7: Which of the following physiological changes occurs in a pregnant woman's respiratory system?

A. Decreased respiratory rate

B. Increased tidal volume

C. Decreased oxygen demand

Q8: Throughout pregnancy, what physiological alteration takes place in a woman's respiratory system?

A. Decrease in respiratory rate

B. Rise in tidal volume

C. Reduction in oxygen demand

Q9 In the later stages of her pregnancy the woman is informed that she has placenta previa Which of the following risk factors occurring before childbirth is linked to this condition?

A. Maternal age over 35 years

B. Multiparity

C. Previous cesarean section

Q10: Obesity is a significant antenatal factor that can impact pregnancy and birth outcomes. Can you please provide more context or information about the relationship between obesity and bariatric surgery during pregnancy?

A. Bariatric surgery is contraindicated during pregnancy due to increased risks.

B. Bariatric surgery reduces the risk of gestational diabetes in obese pregnant women.

C. Bariatric surgery increases the risk of preterm birth in obese pregnant women.

Q11: Fetal heart rate patterns and blood gases are important indicators of fetal well-being and oxygenation during labor. Which fetal heart rate pattern shows a gentle, even drop in the fetal heart rate starting when the contraction begins, and it returns to its usual level by the end of the contraction?

A. Early decelerations

B. Late decelerations

C. Variable decelerations

Q12: A pregnant woman at 37 weeks gestation is experiencing decreased fetal movement. Upon assessing the fetal heart rate, the maternal nurse notes a heart rate of 80 beats per minute. Which fetal heart rate abnormality is most likely occurring in this situation?

A. Tachycardia

B. Bradycardia

C. Altered variability

Maternal Postpartum Assessment, Management, and Education

Q13: During the postpartum period, the healthcare provider is assessing a woman's reproductive system. Which finding would be considered normal for a woman in this phase of her recovery?

A. Lochia rubra with clots

B. Enlarged and tender uterus

C. Persistent cervical dilation

D. Absence of uterine involution

Q14: A postpartum woman reports feeling a sudden onset of shortness of breath, chest pain, and rapid heart rate. Upon assessment the nurse notes increased respiratory rate decreased oxygen saturation and swelling in the lower extremities. Which condition should the nurse suspect in this postpartum woman?

A. Pulmonary embolism

B. Pneumonia

C. Postpartum cardiomyopathy

D. Postpartum hemorrhage

Q15: A postpartum woman reports experiencing excessive sweating, especially at night, since giving birth. Which physiological change during the postpartum period is likely responsible for this symptom?

A. Increased progesterone levels

B. Decreased estrogen levels

C. Changes in thyroid hormone levels

D. Increased prolactin levels

Q16 A 28-year-old postpartum woman presents to the maternity clinic with complaints of burning and pain during urination. She gave birth to a healthy baby boy three days ago. On assessment her vital signs are stable and she has no signs of fever or abdominal pain. Upon further inquiry, she mentions that she has been experiencing increased urinary frequency and urgency. What could be the most likely reason for her symptoms?

A. Urinary tract infection (UTI)

B. Postpartum diuresis

C. Bladder trauma during delivery

D. Urinary retention

Q17: A postpartum woman reports experiencing constipation since giving birth. What is the most suitable method to help promote regular bowel movements after childbirth?

A. Encouraging increased fluid intake and dietary fiber

B. Administering a laxative medication

C. Restricting fluid intake to prevent bladder distention

D. Encouraging bed rest to conserve energy

Q18: A postpartum woman presents with abdominal distension, bloating, and nausea. On assessment, you note absent bowel sounds and a firm, distended abdomen. What condition should you suspect?

A. Paralytic ileus

B. Urinary tract infection

C. Gastroenteritis

D. Incisional hernia

Q19: The Lamaze breathing pattern begins and ends with

A. Slow-paced breath through the mouth

B. Rapid panting breaths

C. Cleansing breaths

Q20: A breastfeeding woman with sore nipples should be advised to take which action to promote healing and alleviate discomfort?

A. Ensure that the infant has a proper latch onto the breast

B. Limit the feeding time on each breast

C. Apply lanolin cream after each feeding

Q21: A postpartum woman who underwent a cesarean section is receiving care in the recovery room. The nurse is monitoring the woman for potential complications. Which assessment finding requires immediate intervention?

A. Incisional pain with a pain score of 5 out of 10

B. Fundus firm and located two fingerbreadths above the umbilicus

C. Temperature of 100.4°F 38°C and chills

Q22: A postpartum woman is diagnosed with postpartum depression PPD. The nurse is providing education to the woman and her partner about PPD and its management. Which statement by the partner indicates understanding of the condition?

A. "I should encourage her to snap out of it and be more positive."

B. "We should seek professional help and consider therapy or medication."

C. "She just needs more rest and time to adjust to motherhood."

Q23: A postpartum woman who has recently delivered is diagnosed with a urinary tract infection UTI. Which class of medication is commonly prescribed to treat UTIs?

A. Insulin

B. Analgesics (Tylenol)

C. Antimicrobials

Q24: A postpartum woman with gestational diabetes requires medication to manage her blood glucose levels. During the postpartum period, which medication is often prescribed as an antidiabetic?

A. Insulin

B. Analgesics (Tylenol)

C. Antimicrobials

Q25: A postpartum woman who has just undergone a vaginal delivery is experiencing excessive postpartum bleeding. Which medication is commonly administered as an oxytocic to control uterine bleeding?

A. Insulin

B. Analgesics (Tylenol)

C. Oxytocic

Q26: A postpartum woman is receiving antiretroviral medication for the management of her HIV infection. She asks the nurse if it is safe for her to receive the influenza vaccine. What is the appropriate response by the nurse?

A. "Yes, it is safe to receive the influenza vaccine while taking antiretroviral medication."

B. "No, you should not receive the influenza vaccine while taking antiretroviral medication."

C. "You should consult your healthcare provider before receiving the influenza vaccine."

Q27: A postpartum woman with gestational diabetes is prescribed insulin. Which statement by the woman indicates understanding of insulin administration?

A. "I should rotate the injection sites to avoid lipodystrophy."

B. "I can adjust the insulin dosage based on my blood sugar levels."

C. "Insulin can be taken orally for better absorption."

Q28: A breastfeeding woman is experiencing postpartum pain and requests analgesics. Which statement by the nurse is appropriate when educating the woman about taking analgesics while breastfeeding?

A. "It is safe to take Tylenol acetaminophen for pain relief while breastfeeding."

B. To ensure safety it is advisable to avoid antimicrobials as they can pass into breast milk.

C. "Diuretics can reduce breast milk production, so it is best to avoid them."

Q29: A postpartum woman complains of severe perineal pain and swelling following a vaginal delivery. The nurse suspects perineal edema and pain. Which nursing intervention is appropriate for managing perineal edema and pain in the postpartum period?

A. Applying ice packs to the perineal area at regular intervals

B. Administering over the counter nonsteroidal anti-inflammatory drugs NSAIDs

C. Encouraging the woman to perform Kegel exercises to promote perineal muscle tone

Q30: A postpartum woman presents with complaints of constipation and difficulty passing stools after childbirth. What nursing intervention is appropriate for managing constipation in the postpartum period?

A. Encouraging increased fluid intake and a high-fiber diet

B. Administering laxatives or stool softeners as prescribed

C. Instructing the woman to avoid physical activity and bed rest

Q31: A postpartum woman reports experiencing intense pain in her perineal area, which worsens when she sits or moves. On assessment, the nurse observes swelling, redness, and warmth in the perineal region. The woman also has a low-grade fever. What complication should the nurse suspect based on these findings?

A. Perineal edema and pain

B. Breast engorgement

C. Vaginal lacerations

Q32: A postpartum woman is concerned about her nutritional needs during breastfeeding. Which statement by the woman indicates a need for further education?

A. "I should increase my fluid intake to support milk production."

B. "I need to consume more calories than I did during pregnancy."

C. "I can rely solely on prenatal vitamins to meet my nutrient needs."

Q33: A postpartum woman asks the nurse about contraception options. Which statement by the woman indicates a need for further education?

A. "I'm considering using a combination hormonal contraceptive."

B. "I'll start using a barrier method like condoms until I decide on a long-term option."

C. "I can start using an intrauterine device IUD immediately after childbirth."

Q34: A lactating mother is concerned about her nutritional needs while breastfeeding. Which statement accurately describes maternal nutritional needs during lactation?

A. "During lactation, mothers require an additional 500 calories per day to support milk production and meet their energy needs."

B. "Maternal nutritional needs remain the same during lactation as they were during pregnancy."

C. "Mothers should restrict their calorie intake during lactation to promote weight loss and achieve their pre-pregnancy body weight."

Q35: A new mother is concerned about the composition of her breast milk. Which statement accurately describes the composition of breast milk?

A. Breast milk is a remarkable fluid that adapts its composition during lactation to cater to the evolving nutritional requirements of the baby.

B. "The composition of breast milk remains constant throughout lactation and is not influenced by maternal or infant factors."

C. "Breast milk contains only basic nutrients such as carbohydrates, proteins, and fats, without any additional bioactive components."

Q36: A new mother is experiencing difficulty with the latch on during breastfeeding. Which key aspect of the normal breastfeeding process should the nurse prioritize in order to improve latch on?

A. Positioning

B. Suck/Swallow/Sequence

C. Timing (Frequency and Duration)

Q37: A breastfeeding mother asks how she can determine if her newborn is getting enough milk during feedings. What should the nurse explain to the mother about feeding cues?

A. Feeding cues are signs that indicate the baby is hungry and ready to feed.

B. Feeding cues are indicators that the baby is full and has had enough milk.

C. Feeding cues are specific time intervals that should be followed for feeding the baby.

Q38: Sarah, a postpartum woman, is experiencing breast engorgement and seeks advice on relieving discomfort through hand expression. She explains that she has been following all the key points of normal hand expression but is still having difficulty obtaining significant milk flow. The nurse assesses Sarah's technique and finds that she is positioning her hand correctly, applying gentle pressure, and following the recommended sequence. The nurse decides to explore other factors that could impact milk removal. Which key point should the nurse emphasize when discussing milk ejection reflex and its influence on effective hand expression?

A. Positioning

B. Feeding Cues

C. Suck/Swallow/Sequence

Q39: A postpartum woman is concerned about her milk supply and wants to increase it. Which key point of breast care should the nurse focus on when providing education and support to the mother?

A. Use of Supplementary Feedings

B. Use of Breastfeeding Devices

C. Expressing and Storing Breast Milk

Q40: A postpartum mother asks about the benefits of using breastfeeding devices. Which key point of breast care should the nurse emphasize when responding to the mother's inquiry?

A. Use of Supplementary Feedings

B. Use of Breastfeeding Devices

C. Expressing and Storing Breast Milk

Q41: A breastfeeding mother is concerned about the size and shape of her nipples affecting her baby's ability to latch properly. Which key point of nipple care should be recommended to assist with infant latching?

A. Using nipple shields to facilitate a better latch

B. Applying lanolin cream to moisturize the nipples

C. Utilizing breast shells to draw out flat or inverted nipples

Q42: A postpartum woman has been diagnosed with active tuberculosis (TB). Which of the following is a contraindication to breastfeeding in this situation?

A. Maternal complications

B. Latch on problems

C. Maternal illness

Q43: A lactating mother has been prescribed a medication that is known to have significant risks for the infant. Which of the following is a contraindication to breastfeeding in this case?

A. Therapeutic medications

B. Breast engorgement

C. Insufficient milk supply

Q44: A mother with postpartum depression is finding it challenging to care for her newborn. The healthcare provider suggests involving the father or another family member in the care of the infant to:

A. Promote maternal-infant bonding

B. Increase maternal sleep deprivation

C. Introduce maternal complications

Q45: A newborn is diagnosed with respiratory distress syndrome and requires supplemental oxygen therapy. Which intervention should the nurse prioritize to prevent complications associated with oxygen therapy?

A. Monitor the newborn's oxygen saturation levels

B. Provide frequent bottle feedings to support growth

C. Administer bronchodilator medications

Q46: A full-term newborn presents with poor muscle tone, lethargy, and feeding difficulties shortly after birth. The healthcare provider suspects a metabolic disorder. Which laboratory test should be prioritized to confirm the diagnosis?

A. Blood glucose level

B. Bilirubin level

C. Blood ammonia level

Q47: A new mother expresses concerns about her ability to meet the needs of her newborn. Which response by the nurse best reflects a normal characteristic of parental self-efficacy during the postpartum period?

A. "It's common to doubt yourself as a parent, but you'll gain confidence with time and experience."

B. "You should consider seeking professional help for your feelings of inadequacy."

C. "Parenting is a challenging task, and most parents never feel truly competent."

Q48: A postpartum nurse is performing an assessment on a woman who recently gave birth. During the assessment, the nurse observes that the woman's fundus is firm, midline, and located two fingerbreadths below the umbilicus. Based on these findings, the nurse determines that the woman's uterus is:

A. Contracting appropriately and involuting.

B. Experiencing atony and requires further evaluation.

C. Retained with placental fragments and needs immediate intervention.

Q49: A nurse is providing education to a woman who is planning to breastfeed her newborn. The nurse discusses the benefits of breastfeeding and emphasizes the importance of proper latch and positioning. Which statement by the woman indicates a need for further teaching?

A. "I should bring my baby's mouth to my breast, making sure to include a large portion of the areola."

B. "It's important to ensure that my baby's lips are flanged outward while breastfeeding."

C. "I can use a pacifier to help soothe my baby if they are having difficulty latching."

Q50: A postpartum nurse is conducting a sibling visitation session for a family with a new baby. The nurse observes the older sibling showing signs of anxiety and reluctance to interact with the newborn. Which intervention would be most appropriate for the nurse to facilitate a positive sibling visitation experience?

A. Encouraging the older sibling to hold the newborn without any assistance.

B. Allowing the older sibling to choose a small gift for the newborn as a gesture of acceptance.

C. Instructing the older sibling to keep a distance from the newborn until they feel more comfortable.

Q51: A postpartum nurse is providing guidance to a woman who is experiencing challenges in establishing breastfeeding and worries about the impact on parent/infant interactions. Which statement by the nurse accurately addresses the impact of breastfeeding difficulties on parent/infant interactions?

A. "Breastfeeding difficulties have no effect on parent/infant interactions."

B. "Switching to formula feeding will improve parent/infant interactions."

C. "Seeking support from a lactation consultant can help overcome breastfeeding challenges and enhance parent/infant interactions."

Q52: A postpartum nurse is conducting a home visit for a family with a newborn. The nurse observes cluttered living conditions and limited space, potentially impacting family integration. Which intervention would be most appropriate for the nurse to facilitate a supportive environment for the family?

A. Recommending the family to minimize personal belongings to create more space.

B. Assisting the family in organizing and decluttering their living environment.

C. Advising the family to prioritize individual spaces over shared spaces.

Q53: A postpartum nurse is providing education on cultural factors influencing family integration to a group of nursing students. The nurse discusses the concept of acculturation and its impact on family dynamics. Which statement accurately describes the influence of acculturation on family integration?

A. "Acculturation has a minimal effect on family integration as individuals maintain their cultural identity."

B. "Acculturation often leads to complete assimilation into the dominant culture, erasing cultural differences."

C. "Acculturation can result in a blend of cultural values and practices that impact family integration."

Q54: A postpartum nurse is educating a group of healthcare providers on screening for intimate partner violence. Which statement accurately reflects the importance of universal screening?

A. "Universal screening for intimate partner violence is unnecessary as victims will disclose abuse if they feel comfortable."

B. "Universal screening helps identify cases of intimate partner violence that may otherwise go undetected."

C. "Healthcare providers should only screen for intimate partner violence if there are visible signs of physical abuse."

Q55: A nurse is conducting a postpartum education session for a group of new parents. One mother asks about the potential impact of substance use during pregnancy on the newborn. Which response by the nurse is most accurate and informative?

A. "Substance use during pregnancy can lead to neonatal abstinence syndrome NA which causes withdrawal symptoms in the newborn."

B. "If a mother used substances during pregnancy, the newborn will likely have long-term developmental delays."

C. Substance use during pregnancy has limited effects and does not pose significant risks to the newborn.

Q56: A couple who has adopted a newborn is seeking guidance on how to support the child's future exploration of their adoption story. Which advice should the nurse provide to promote healthy family dynamics?

A. Encourage open and age-appropriate communication about adoption throughout the child's development.

B. Discourage the child from exploring their adoption story to prevent confusion or distress.

C. Keep the child's adoption a secret until they are older and better able to understand.

Q57: A mother is experiencing perinatal grief after the loss of her newborn. Which intervention by the nurse is most appropriate to facilitate the mother's healing process?

A. Encouraging the mother to express her feelings and emotions openly in a supportive environment.

B. Discouraging the mother from seeking support from friends and family to avoid dependency.

C. Minimizing discussions about the baby to help the mother move on from her loss.

Q58: A nurse is involved in the decision-making process regarding the allocation of limited resources in the postpartum unit. Which ethical principle should guide the nurse's actions in ensuring fair distribution of resources?

A. Autonomy

B. Beneficence

C. Justice

Q59: A newborn has a birth weight of 4.2 kg (9.3 lbs.) and exhibits signs of hypoglycemia, such as jitteriness and poor feeding. What condition is most likely causing these symptoms?

A. Large for gestational age (LGA)

B. Small for gestational age (SGA)

C. Gestational diabetes

Q60: A nurse is conducting a newborn hearing screening using the otoacoustic emissions (OAE) test. What does a "pass" result on the OAE test indicate?

A. Normal hearing function

B. Possible hearing impairment

C. Further testing is required

Q61: A newborn is experiencing heat loss through evaporation. Which intervention would be most effective in reducing evaporative heat loss?

A. Drying the newborn thoroughly immediately after birth.

B. Keeping the newborn in a warm room temperature environment.

C. Wrapping the newborn in a warm blanket.

Q62: A nurse is reviewing a newborn's laboratory results and notes a low platelet count. What condition should the nurse suspect?

A. Polycythemia

B. Thrombocytosis

C. Thrombocytopenia

Q63: A newborn is suspected to have a metabolic disorder. Which laboratory test would be most useful in confirming the diagnosis?

A. Blood glucose level

B. Blood gas analysis

C. Ammonia level

Q64: A nurse is performing a gestational age assessment on a newborn using the New Ballard Score. Which finding is associated with a preterm newborn?

A. Well-formed external genitalia

B. Noticing deep creases on the soles of the feet.

C. Minimal presence of lanugo on the body

Q65: A newborn is assessed using the Dubowitz/Ballard Assessment to determine gestational age. Which finding suggests a post-term newborn?

A. Flat areolae without buds

B. Thin, wrinkled skin with visible veins

C. Recoiled and firm ear cartilage

Q67: During a neurobehavioral assessment, a newborn demonstrates smooth, coordinated movements while turning the head to one side. What reflex is being assessed?

A. Rooting reflex

B. Galant reflex

C. Tonic neck reflex

Q67: A nurse is conducting a sensory assessment on a newborn and observes a strong withdrawal response when a finger is lightly touched on the sole of the foot. What reflex is being assessed?

A. Babinski reflex

B. Moro reflex

C. Plantar grasp reflex

Q68: A predisposing factor for assisted delivery (forceps or vacuum) is:

A. Adolescent pregnancy

B. Multiparity

C. Postdates gestation

Q69: A parent asks the nurse about signs of infection to watch for in the umbilical cord stump. Which signs should the nurse include in the response?

A. Redness, swelling, and a small amount of clear drainage

B. Yellow discharge and mild tenderness

C. Increased redness, warmth, and purulent discharge from the stump

Q70: The nurse is assessing a newborn's urine output. Which finding would be considered abnormal and require further evaluation?

A. Pale yellow urine

B. 10 wet diapers in a 24-hour period

C. Urine with a strong ammonia odor

Q71: A nurse is providing education to parents about post-circumcision care for their newborn. Which instruction should the nurse include?

A. Cleanse the circumcision site with hydrogen peroxide twice a day.

B. Apply petroleum jelly to the circumcision site after each diaper change.

C. Avoid using diapers or covering the circumcision site to allow air exposure.

Q72: A parent asks the nurse about techniques to soothe their newborn during a bath. Which recommendation should the nurse provide?

A. Maintain a warm room temperature during the bath to prevent chilling.

B. Use a sponge bath instead of immersing the newborn in water.

C. Delay the first bath until the umbilical cord stump falls off.

Q73: A nurse is providing education to parents about non-pharmacological pain management for their newborn. Which technique should the nurse include?

A. Kangaroo care (skin-to-skin contact) to promote comfort and bonding.

B. Applying a topical anesthetic cream to the newborn's skin before painful procedures.

C. Administering over the counter pain relievers as directed by the healthcare provider.

Q74: A nurse is providing education to parents about car seat safety for their newborn. Which statement by the parents indicates understanding of the information?

A. "We should secure the car seat using the vehicle's seat belt rather than the LATCH system."

B. "We can place the car seat in the front seat as long as the airbag is turned off."

C. "We should avoid using aftermarket accessories or modifications with the car seat."

Q75: A parent asks the nurse about the appropriate position of the car seat harness on their newborn. What is the nurse's best response?

A. "The car seat harness should be positioned at or below the newborn's shoulders."

B. "The car seat harness should be positioned above the newborn's shoulders."

C. "The car seat harness should be positioned loosely to allow for movement."

Q76: A nurse is providing education to parents about newborn sun protection. What should the nurse include as a sun safety measure?

A. Keeping the newborn out of direct sunlight and using protective clothing

B. Applying sunscreen with a high SPF directly to the newborn's skin

C. Allowing the newborn to spend long periods of time in direct sunlight to promote vitamin D synthesis

Q77: A parent asks the nurse about managing newborn skin rashes. What is the nurse's best response?

A. "If the rash persists or worsens, consult the healthcare provider for further evaluation and treatment."

B. "Apply a topical steroid cream to the affected areas to reduce inflammation."

C. "Use over-the-counter antihistamines to alleviate itching and discomfort."

Q78: A nurse is discussing safe sleep practices with parents. Which action should the nurse recommend for reducing the risk of suffocation in the newborn's sleep area?

A. Keeping the sleep area free from loose bedding, pillows, and stuffed animals

B. Using a firm pillow under the newborn's head for added comfort

C. Co-sleeping with the newborn to provide warmth and security

Q79: A parent asks the nurse about the appropriate sleep position for their newborn. What is the nurse's best response?

A. "Always place your newborn to sleep on their back to reduce the risk of SIDS."

B. "Sleeping on the side is safe and provides better airflow for the newborn."

C. "Letting the newborn choose their preferred sleep position is best."

Q80: A nurse is administering hepatitis B immunoglobulin (HBIG) to a newborn. What is the purpose of administering HBIG?

A. To provide immediate passive immunity against hepatitis B virus

B. To boost the newborn's natural immune response to hepatitis B

C. To prevent respiratory infections and improve lung function in the newborn

Q81: A newborn is receiving a dose of analgesic medication for pain relief. What is the primary action of analgesics in newborns?

A. To block pain signals and reduce pain perception in the central nervous system

B. To stimulate the production of endorphins and promote feelings of wellbeing

C. To relax muscles and reduce muscle tension in the newborn

Q82: A newborn is born with a heart rate of 120 beats per minute and good respiratory effort. The newborn is receiving positive-pressure ventilation and the heart rate remains stable. What is the appropriate next step?

A. Continue positive-pressure ventilation

B. Administer epinephrine intravenously

C. Initiate chest compressions

Q83: A newborn is born with a heart rate of 60 beats per minute despite adequate ventilation and chest compressions. What intervention should be performed?

A. Administer sodium bicarbonate intravenously

B. Administer normal saline bolus

C. Initiate advanced cardiac life support (ACLS) guidelines

Q84: What is the primary objective of administering epinephrine during newborn resuscitation?

A. Improving heart rate

B. Increasing respiratory effort

C. Restoring normal blood glucose levels

Q85: During the resuscitation of a newborn, what is the immediate action if the newborn remains apneic and has a heart rate of 0 beats per minute despite adequate ventilation and chest compressions?

A. Administering epinephrine intravenously

B. Initiating advanced cardiac life support (ACLS) guidelines

C. Continuing ventilation and chest compressions

Q86: In the treatment of neonatal seizures, which medication is commonly used as a first-line therapy?

A. Phenobarbital

B. Naloxone

C. Albuterol

Q87: What medication is typically administered to newborns as a preventive measure against respiratory syncytial virus RSV infection?

A. Palivizumab

B. Gentamicin

C. Amphotericin B

Q88: A newborn with persistent hypotension was started on intravenous fluids. What finding indicates the effectiveness of the intervention?

A. Decreased urine output

B. Increased blood pressure

C. Worsening edema

Q89: A newborn with meconium aspiration syndrome received endotracheal suctioning. What finding suggests that the intervention was effective?

A. Increased respiratory distress

B. Decreased oxygen saturation

C. Improved breath sounds

Q90: The Apgar score primarily assesses a newborn's:

A. Physical maturity

B. Neurologic function

C. Respiratory status

Q91: A newborn scores 6 on the Apgar scale at 1 minute after birth and 8 at 5 minutes. What does this change in score indicate?

A. The newborn's condition is improving.

B. The newborn's condition is deteriorating.

C. The score is within the normal range, no significant change.

Q92: The nurse should closely monitor the woman for signs and symptoms of hypovolemic shock in cases of severe postpartum hemorrhage. These may include:

A. Weak and thread pulse

B. Increased urine output

C. Elevated blood pressure

Q93: In cases of postpartum hemorrhage, the administration of packed red blood cells may be necessary to:

A. Increase oxygen-carrying capacity

B. Promote uterine contraction

C. Correct coagulation disorders

Q94: The nurse should instruct the woman with postpartum thrombophlebitis to avoid which of the following?

A. Prolonged sitting or standing

B. Physical activity and exercise

C. Deep breathing and coughing exercises

Q95: What is an essential intervention to prevent postpartum thrombophlebitis?

A. Early ambulation

B. Bed rest

C. Restricting fluid intake

Q96: The nurse should educate the postpartum woman about the signs and symptoms of thrombophlebitis, which include:

A. Swelling and tenderness in the affected leg

B. Increased appetite and weight gain

C. Decreased urine output and dark-colored urine

A. Hemorrhage **Q97: The nurse should monitor the postpartum woman with pulmonary embolus for signs of:**

B. Hypertension

C. Respiratory distress

Q98: The primary goal of nursing care for a woman with pulmonary embolus is to:

A. Improve oxygenation and prevent further clot formation

B. Control pain and discomfort

C. Promote relaxation and stress reduction

Correct answer: A. Improve oxygenation and prevent further clot formation

Q99: Nursing interventions for a woman with DIC include:

A. Monitoring vital signs and laboratory values

B. Encouraging ambulation and physical activity

C. Administering anticoagulant medications

Q100: The priority nursing action for a woman with DIC experiencing active bleeding is:

A. Applying direct pressure to the bleeding site

B. Administering blood products

C. Initiating intravenous fluid therapy

Q101: The risk factors for developing HELLP syndrome include:

A. Advanced maternal age

B. Multiple gestation

C. History of smoking

Q102: The long-term complications associated with HELLP syndrome include:

A. Liver failure

B. Chronic hypertension

C. Gestational diabetes

Q103: A large perineal hematoma may result in:

A. Hemorrhagic shock

B. Deep vein thrombosis

C. Bladder injury

Q104: Hematomas can occur in different areas of the body. Which type of hematoma occurs within the breast tissue after childbirth?

A. Subcutaneous hematoma

B. Intracranial hematoma

C. Subareolar hematoma

Q105: Which of the following is a potential complication of a subareolar hematoma?

A. Breast abscess

B. Pulmonary embolism

C. Urinary tract infection

Q106: Women with chronic hypertension should be advised to:

A. Limit caffeine intake

B. Avoid prenatal vitamins

C. Skip regular prenatal visits

Q107: In severe cases of chronic hypertension, early delivery may be recommended to:

A. Reduce the risk of placental abruption

B. Prevent postpartum hemorrhage

C. Facilitate breastfeeding

Q108: Women with chronic hypertension may require additional monitoring during labor, including:

A. Continuous fetal heart rate monitoring

B. Limited fluid intake

C. Administration of oxytocin for labor augmentation

Q109: Women with gestational hypertension should be advised to:

A. Reduce their sodium intake

B. Avoid physical activity

C. Stop taking their prenatal vitamins

Q110: Gestational hypertension increases the risk of developing:

A. Gestational trophoblastic disease

B. Intrauterine growth restriction

C. Neonatal sepsis

Q111: Maternal management during an eclamptic seizure includes:

A. Restraining the woman to prevent injury

B. Placing a padded tongue blade between the teeth

C. Administering oxygen via face mask

Q112: After an eclamptic seizure, maternal vital signs should be monitored, including:

A. Blood pressure

B. Fetal heart rate

C. Respiratory rate

Q113: Complications of untreated or severe endometritis include:

A. Pelvic inflammatory disease (PID)

B. Deep vein thrombosis (DVT)

C. Cervical dysplasia

Q114: The most important nursing intervention for a woman with endometritis is:

A. Promoting adequate hydration

B. Encouraging ambulation

C. Providing emotional support

Q115: Prevention strategies for wound infections include:

A. Proper hand hygiene

B. Early initiation of breastfeeding

C. Limiting physical activity during the postpartum period

Q116: Follow-up care for a woman with a wound infection includes:

A. Assessing for signs of improvement or worsening infection

B. Referral to a lactation consultant

C. Contraceptive counseling

Q117: The most effective method of preventing wound infections is:

A. Appropriate sterile technique during delivery and postpartum care

B. Routine use of antiseptic vaginal washes

C. Timely administration of oxytocin after delivery

Q118: Prevention strategies for septic pelvic thrombophlebitis include:

A. Early mobilization and ambulation

B. Exclusive formula feeding

C. Prophylactic anticoagulation

Q119: Follow-up care for a woman with septic pelvic thrombophlebitis includes:

A. Assessing for resolution of symptoms

B. Referral to a lactation consultant

C. Contraceptive counseling

Q120: The prognosis for septic pelvic thrombophlebitis is generally good with:

A. Early recognition and treatment

B. Prolonged bed rest

C. Surgical intervention

Q121: The most common route of infection leading to a postpartum UTI is:

A. Ascending from the urethra

B. Hematogenous spread

C. Direct contact with contaminated objects

Q122: Follow-up care for a woman with a postpartum UTI includes:

A. Assessing for resolution of symptoms

B. Referral to a lactation consultant

C. Contraceptive counseling

Q123: Women with recurrent UTIs may benefit from:

A. Prophylactic antibiotic use

B. Voiding before and after sexual intercourse

C. Increased fluid intake

Q124: Infants born to mothers with gestational diabetes are at an increased risk of developing which of the following conditions after birth?

A. Hypoglycemia

B. Hyperbilirubinemia

C. Respiratory distress syndrome

Q125: Women with gestational diabetes are encouraged to breastfeed their infants. How does breastfeeding benefit both the mother and the baby?

A. Helps with weight loss in the mother

B. Regulates the baby's blood glucose levels

C. Provides immunity against infections

Q126: Postpartum sleep disturbances are most commonly experienced during which timeframe?

A. The first week after childbirth

B. The first month after childbirth

C. The first three months after childbirth

Q127: Which of the following strategies may help postpartum women establish a regular sleep routine?

A. Irregular sleep-wake schedule

B. Avoiding napping during the day

C. Going to bed and waking up at consistent times

Q128: Postpartum women with sleep disturbances should be encouraged to seek support from healthcare professionals if:

A. Sleep disturbances persist beyond the first month

B. They experience occasional restless sleep

C. They are able to function adequately during the day

Q129: Women with postpartum depression may experience thoughts of self-harm or harm to their infants. What is the appropriate nursing action in this situation?

A. Assuring the woman that these thoughts are normal and will pass

B. Encouraging the woman to keep these thoughts to herself

C. Immediately notifying the healthcare provider and implementing appropriate safety measures

Q130: Postpartum depression can impact the entire family unit. Which of the following interventions promotes family involvement and support?

A. Encouraging the father/partner to take full responsibility for infant care

B. Referring the family to community resources and support groups

C. Advising the family to avoid discussing the mother's depression

Q131: Follow-up care for women with postpartum depression is crucial. What statement about postpartum depression is accurate?

A. Postpartum depression will resolve on its own without any intervention.

B. Experiencing postpartum depression Doesn't pose a significant possibility for future mental health problems.

C. Early identification or treatment of postpartum depression improve outcomes for both the mother and infant.

Q132: When providing care for a pregnant woman with substance use disorder, it is important to involve a multidisciplinary team. Which healthcare professionals are essential to include in the team?

A. Obstetrician only

B. Obstetrician and social worker

C. Obstetrician, social worker, and addiction specialist

Q133 Harm reduction strategies can be implemented to minimize the negative consequences of substance use during pregnancy. Can you provide an example of a harm reduction approach among the following options?

A. Forcing the woman to quit substance use abruptly

B. Providing clean needles to pregnant women who inject drugs

C. Stigmatizing and punishing women who use substances

Q134: Surgical intervention is often required to correct cyanotic heart defects. Which of the following surgical procedures is commonly performed to repair Tetralogy of Fallot?

A. Atrial septal defect (ASD) closure

B. Pulmonary valve replacement

C. Total anomalous pulmonary venous connection (TAPVC) repair

Q135: Surgical intervention is often necessary to correct cyanotic heart disease in newborns. Which of the following surgical procedures is commonly performed to repair Tetralogy of Fallot?

A. Atrial septal defect (ASD) closure

B. Ventricular septal defect (VSD) repair

C. Blalock-Taussig shunt

Q136: Transposition of the great arteries (TGA) is a cyanotic heart defect where the aorta and pulmonary artery are switched. Which of the following statements about TGA is correct?

A. TGA results in increased pulmonary blood flow.

B. TGA is characterized by a ventricular septal defect (VSD).

C. TGA requires immediate surgical intervention after birth.

Q137: A newborn is suspected to have a cyanotic heart disease. Which diagnostic tool is commonly used to evaluate the structure and function of the heart in these cases?

A. Electrocardiogram (ECG)

B. Chest X-ray

C. Echocardiogram

Q138: A nurse is assessing a term newborn for signs of apnea. Which of the following clinical manifestations is commonly associated with apnea in newborns?

A. Cyanosis and bradycardia

B. Hyperactivity and increased heart rate

C. Hypertension and rapid breathing

Q139: A nurse is educating parents about caring for a newborn diagnosed with Transient Tachypnea of the Newborn (TTN). Which of the following statements accurately describes TTN to the parents?

A. "TTN is a long-term respiratory disorder that will require lifelong treatment."

B. "TTN is a temporary condition that typically resolves within a few days after birth."

C. "TTN is a contagious respiratory infection that can be transmitted to family members."

Q140 A nurse is educating parents about caring for a newborn diagnosed with pneumothorax. Which of the following statements accurately describes pneumothorax to the parents?

A. "Pneumothorax is a common infection that can be easily treated with antibiotics."

B. "Pneumothorax is a condition where the baby is lungs collapse due to the accumulation of air."

C. "Pneumothorax is a genetic disorder inherited from one and both parents."

Q141: A nurse is providing education to parents about meconium aspiration syndrome. Which of the following statements accurately describes meconium aspiration to the parents?

A. "Meconium aspiration is a permanent lung condition that will affect your baby's breathing long-term."

B. "Meconium aspiration is a treatable condition, and most babies recover without long-term complications."

C. "Meconium aspiration is a contagious respiratory infection that can spread to other family members."

Q142: A nurse is educating parents about seizures in newborns. Which of the following statements accurately describes seizures to the parents?

A. "Seizures in newborns are a normal part of brain development and will resolve on their own."

B. "Seizures in newborns require immediate medical attention as they can be a sign of a serious underlying condition."

C. "Seizures in newborns are common and can be managed by home remedies and natural treatments."

Q143: A nurse is providing education to parents about jitteriness in newborns. Which of the following statements accurately describes jitteriness to the parents?

A. "Jitteriness in newborns is a normal behavior and will resolve on its own over time."

B. "Jitteriness in newborns is a sign of gastrointestinal issues and can be managed with dietary changes."

C. "Jitteriness in newborns can be a manifestation of an underlying medical condition and requires medical evaluation."

Q144: A nurse is providing education to parents about intracranial hemorrhage in newborns. Which of the following statements accurately describes intracranial hemorrhage to the parents?

A. "Intracranial hemorrhage is a common occurrence in all newborns or does not require any medical attention."

B. "Intracranial hemorrhage can have severe consequences so early medical intervention is crucial."

C. "Intracranial hemorrhage is a benign condition that resolves on its own without any intervention."

Q145: A nurse is conducting a prenatal assessment for a pregnant woman. Which of the following findings should be reported promptly to the healthcare provider due to its association with an increased risk of neural tube defects?

A. Family history of asthma

B. Previous pregnancy with preterm birth

C Maternal use of certain medications, such as isotretinoin Accutane

Q146: A newborn is diagnosed with neonatal abstinence syndrome (NAS) due to maternal substance abuse during pregnancy. Which of the following interventions should the nurse prioritize in the care of this newborn?

A. Implementing a quiet and calm environment

B. Initiating formula feeding to support growth

C. Administering sedative medications for symptom relief

Q147: A nurse is assessing a newborn and suspects the presence of malrotation with volvulus. Which of the following clinical manifestations would the nurse expect to observe in this newborn?

A. Abdominal distension and bilious vomiting

B. Failure to pass meconium and rectal bleeding

C. Painless rectal prolapse and constipation

Q148: A newborn is diagnosed with Hirschsprung's disease. Which of the following symptoms would the nurse expect to observe in this newborn?

A. Abdominal distension and failure to pass meconium

B. Projectile vomiting and irritability

C. Bilious vomiting and bloody stools

Q149: A newborn is diagnosed with sickle cell anemia. Which intervention is essential in the care of this newborn?

A. Administering intravenous antibiotics

B. Providing pain management

C. Monitoring oxygen saturation levels

Q150: A nurse is educating parents about the importance of vitamin K supplementation for their newborn. Which statement by the parents indicates understanding of the teaching?

A. "Vitamin K is necessary for the production of red blood cells in our baby."

B. "Administering vitamin K will help prevent bleeding problems in our baby."

C. "We need to limit our baby's vitamin K intake to prevent toxicity."

Q151: A nurse is caring for a newborn receiving vitamin K supplementation. Which assessment finding indicates an appropriate response to the supplementation?

A. Decreased jaundice

B. Improved feeding pattern

C. Resolution of bruising

Q152: A nurse is providing discharge education to the parents of a newborn with a history of hyperbilirubinemia. Which instruction should the nurse include?

A. "Monitor your baby's urine output and report any changes to the healthcare provider."

B. "Avoid exposing your baby to natural sunlight to prevent further jaundice."

C. "Discontinue breastfeeding to minimize the possibility of recurrent hyperbilirubinemia."

Q153: Which clinical manifestation is commonly seen in a newborn with ABO incompatibility?

A. Jaundice

B. Petechiae

C. Respiratory distress

D. Cyanosis

Q154: What is the recommended management for a newborn with ABO incompatibility presenting with significant hyperbilirubinemia?

A. Phototherapy

B. Exchange transfusion

C. Supportive care and monitoring

Q155: What is the recommended treatment for severe hemolytic disease of the newborn?

A. Phototherapy

B. Exchange transfusion

C. Intravenous immunoglobulin IVIG administration

Q156: Which of the following triggers can lead to a hemolytic crisis in individuals with G6PD deficiency?

A. Fava beans (broad beans)

B. Citrus fruits

C. Dairy products

Q157: Which laboratory test is used to diagnose G6PD deficiency?

A. Complete blood count (CBC)

B. Coombs test

C. G6PD enzyme assay

Q158: A nurse is caring for a neonate with polycythemia. Which clinical finding is consistent with this condition?

A. Cyanosis of the extremities

B. Tachypnea and grunting

C. Poor weight gain

Q159: Which maternal factor is associated with an increased risk of polycythemia in the newborn?

A. Maternal diabetes

B. Maternal hypertension

C. Maternal anemia

Q160: Which intervention should the nurse prioritize to prevent complications in a neonate with hyper viscosity?

A. Administering intravenous fluids

B. Performing frequent blood transfusions

C. Monitoring for signs of infection

Q161: Which intervention should the nurse prioritize to prevent complications in a neonate with thrombocytopenia?

A. Administering platelet transfusions

B. Monitoring for signs of infection

C. Providing phototherapy for jaundice

Q162: Which intervention should the nurse prioritize for a neonate with suspected neonatal sepsis?

A. Administering broad-spectrum antibiotics

B. Providing phototherapy for hyperbilirubinemia

C. Initiating respiratory support with nasal cannula

Q163: A nurse is caring for a newborn with an elevated WBC count and neutrophilia on the CBC. What intervention should the nurse anticipate?

A. Initiating antibiotics

B. Administering antiviral medication

C. Initiating antipyretic therapy

Q164: A newborn's CBC shows thrombocytopenia. Which intervention should the nurse prioritize?

A. Administering platelet transfusions

B. Monitoring for signs of bleeding

C. Providing phototherapy for jaundice

Q165: A nurse is caring for a newborn following a lumbar puncture. Which assessment finding would require immediate intervention?

A. Mild headache

B. Clear drainage from the puncture site

C. Irritability and inconsolable crying

Q166: What is the most appropriate nursing action immediately after a lumbar puncture in a newborn?

A. Apply pressure to the puncture site

B. Place the newborn in a prone position

C. Monitor the newborn's vital signs every 15 minutes

Q167: A newborn is diagnosed with congenital rubella syndrome What are some common findings or symptoms often associated with this condition?

A. Micrognathia (small jaw)

B. Webbed neck

C. Clubfoot

Q168: A pregnant woman is diagnosed with genital herpes. What intervention is recommended during labor to reduce the risk of neonatal herpes transmission?

A. Administration of antiviral medications to the woman during labor

B. Performing a cesarean section to avoid vaginal delivery

C. Monitoring the woman's viral load during labor

Q169: A newborn is diagnosed with hepatitis B infection. What intervention is recommended to prevent transmission of hepatitis B to the newborn?

A. Administering the hepatitis B vaccine to the newborn

B. Administering antiviral medications to the newborn

C. Isolating the newborn in a separate room

Q170: A newborn is diagnosed with congenital syphilis and requires treatment with penicillin How is penicillin typically given for treating congenital syphilis?

A. Intravenous (IV) infusion

B. Intramuscular (IM) injection

C. Oral administration

Q171 During pregnancy, a woman with a history of HIV infection needs antiretroviral therapy ART What medication is frequently used as part of ART to lower the risk of perinatal HIV transmission?

A. Zidovudine

B. Efavirenz

C. Lamivudine

Q172: Which of the following maternal risk factors increases the likelihood of a newborn developing hypoglycemia?

A. Obesity

B. Hypothyroidism

C. Preeclampsia

Q173: Which of the following is a screening test commonly used to detect inborn errors of metabolism in newborns?

A. Blood culture

B. Newborn blood spot screening (heel prick)

C. Lumbar puncture

Q174: A couple is concerned about the recurrence risk of a genetic condition in their future pregnancies. The genetic counselor explains that if the condition follows an autosomal recessive inheritance pattern, what is the chance that their subsequent child will be affected if their first child is affected?

A. 0%

B. 25%

C. 50%

Q175: Why are infants of diabetic mothers at higher risk of developing hypoglycemia shortly after birth?

A. Maternal hyperglycemia leads to excess insulin production in the fetus.

B. Maternal hypoglycemia reduces glucose transfer to the fetus.

C. Maternal diabetes causes decreased glycogen stores in the fetus.

Test 4 Answer Key

1	B	27	A	53	C
2	C	28	A	54	B
3	A	29	A	55	A
4	A	30	A	56	A
5	C	31	C	57	A
6	A	32	C	58	C
7	B	33	C	59	A
8	B	34	A	60	A
9	C	35	A	61	A
10	A	36	A	62	C
11	A	37	A	63	C
12	B	38	B	64	C
13	B	39	C	65	B
14	A	40	B	66	C
15	B	41	C	67	A
16	A	42	C	68	C
17	A	43	A	69	C
18	A	44	A	70	C
19	C	45	A	71	B
20	A	46	C	72	B
21	C	47	A	73	A
22	B	48	A	74	C
23	C	49	C	75	A
24	A	50	B	76	A
25	C	51	C	77	A
26	A	52	B	78	A

79	A	106	A	133	B
80	A	107	A	134	B
81	A	108	A	135	B
82	A	109	A	136	B
83	C	110	B	137	C
84	A	111	C	138	A
85	B	112	A	139	B
86	A	113	A	140	B
87	A	114	A	141	B
88	B	115	A	142	B
89	C	116	A	143	C
90	C	117	A	144	B
91	A	118	A	145	C
92	A	119	A	146	A
93	A	120	A	147	A
94	A	121	A	148	A
95	A	122	A	149	B
96	A	123	B	150	B
97	C	124	A	151	C
98	A	125	B	152	A
99	A	126	B	153	A
100	A	127	C	154	C
101	B	128	A	155	B
102	B	129	C	156	A
103	A	130	B	157	C
104	C	131	C	158	A
105	A	132	C	159	A

160	A	166	C	172	A
161	A	167	A	173	B
162	A	168	B	174	B
163	A	169	A	175	A
164	B	170	B		
165	C	171	A		

Maternal Newborn Nursing Exam Practice Test 5

Q1: A pregnant woman has been diagnosed with gestational diabetes mellitus GDM. Which of the following interventions is essential to manage GDM and promote a healthy pregnancy?

A. Limiting fluid intake during the day

B. Monitoring blood pressure regularly

C. Following a well-balanced diet and monitoring blood glucose levels

Q 2: During an antenatal assessment, a 39-year-old pregnant woman expresses concerns about potential risks associated with her age. Which maternal factor is the primary consideration for women of advanced maternal age during pregnancy?

A. Previous cesarean section

B. Multifetal gestation

C. Increased risk of chromosomal abnormalities

Q3: During an antenatal assessment, a pregnant woman asks about the importance of proper nutrition during pregnancy. Which nutrient is essential for fetal neural tube development and is recommended for supplementation before and during early pregnancy?

A. Vitamin C

B. Iron

C. Folic acid

Q4: During an antenatal visit, a pregnant woman provides her obstetrical history, and the nurse identifies a potential risk factor. Which obstetrical history factor may increase the risk of preterm labor and delivery in subsequent pregnancies?

A. History of previous cesarean section

B. History of gestational diabetes mellitus GDM

C. History of preterm birth in a previous pregnancy

Q5: During an antenatal assessment, a pregnant woman discloses feelings of anxiety and uncertainty about her cultural practices conflicting with modern healthcare practices. Which psychosocial/cultural issue is essential for the nurse to address to provide culturally sensitive care?

A. Religious beliefs and practices related to childbirth

B. Preferences for birthing positions and labor support

C. Cultural dietary restrictions during pregnancy

Q6: A couple has been trying to conceive for over a year without success. They are seeking fertility evaluation and treatment. What antenatal factor is the primary concern in their situation?

A. Previous history of preeclampsia

B. Advanced maternal age

C. Infertility

Q7: During an antenatal assessment, a pregnant woman asks about the physiological changes she can expect during pregnancy. Which physiological change is a normal adaptation to pregnancy that helps increase blood volume to support fetal growth?

A. Decreased heart rate

B. Decreased red blood cell count

C. Increased plasma volume

Q8: A pregnant woman with a history of chronic hypertension is at an increased risk of developing a serious antepartum complication. Which antepartum possibility factor should the healthcare provider closely monitor to detect this complication?

A. Gestational diabetes mellitus (GDM)

B. Ectopic pregnancy

C. Preeclampsia

Q9: In her current pregnancy, a woman with a history of two previous cesarean sections shares her wish for a vaginal birth. What antepartum complication should the healthcare provider consider when evaluating the woman's eligibility for a vaginal birth after cesarean (VBAC)?

A. Preterm labor

B. Placenta previa

C. Gestational diabetes mellitus (GDM)

Q10: A pregnant woman at 36 weeks of gestation is scheduled for a non-stress test NST to assess fetal well-being. What does the NST primarily evaluate?

A. Fetal heart rate variability

B. Fetal lung maturity

C. Fetal position in the uterus

Q11: A pregnant woman who underwent bariatric surgery in the past presents for antenatal care. Which complication should the healthcare provider monitor closely due to the woman's history of bariatric surgery?

A. Gestational diabetes mellitus (GDM)

B. Iron deficiency anemia

C. Ectopic pregnancy

Q12: During labor, the fetal heart rate (FHR) pattern indicates late decelerations on the monitor strip. What does this pattern signify, and what immediate nursing intervention is required?

A. Late decelerations indicate uteroplacental insufficiency, and the nurse should position the mother on her left side, administer oxygen, and notify the healthcare provider.

B. Late decelerations indicate fetal distress, and the nurse should prepare for an emergency cesarean section.

C. Late decelerations indicate normal fetal adaptation to labor, and no intervention is required.

Q13 During the postpartum period, a woman's uterus undergoes changes to return to its non-pregnant state. What do we call the process where the uterus gradually decreases in size?

A. Uterine atrophy

B. Uterine involution

C. Uterine regression

Q14: During the postpartum period, a woman's cardiac output returns to its non-pregnant level. What physiological change contributes to the normalization of cardiac output?

A. Increased heart rate

B. Increased stroke volume

C. Decreased blood volume

Q15: Which of the following physical assessment findings is considered a normal respiratory change in the postpartum woman?

A. Increased respiratory rate

B. Increased breath sounds

C. Decreased chest expansion

Q16: During the postpartum period women may experience changes in their genitourinary system. What are some typical physiological changes often seen during the postpartum period?

A. Increased urinary output

B. Decreased bladder capacity

C. Decreased vaginal bleeding

Q17: During the postpartum period, many women may experience changes in their gastrointestinal system. Which of the following gastrointestinal changes is commonly observed in the postpartum period?

A. Increased appetite

B. Constipation

C. Decreased gastric acidity

Q18: A postpartum woman complains of abdominal pain or cramping during the postpartum period. Which of the following interventions should the nurse recommend to alleviate the woman's discomfort?

A. Encouraging the woman to avoid ambulation

B. Administering intravenous pain medication

C. Providing warm compresses to the abdomen

Q19: During the postpartum period, which of the following hematological changes is commonly observed in women?

A. Increased red blood cell count

B. Decreased white blood cell count

C. Physiological anemia

Q20: During the postpartum period, which endocrine gland undergoes an involution process, returning to its pre-pregnancy size?

A. Thyroid gland

B. Adrenal gland

C. Pituitary gland

Q21 A postpartum woman who has undergone a cesarean section requires close monitoring and nursing care to prevent complications. During the postoperative care of a woman after a cesarean section, which interventions should the nurse focus on as a priority?

A. Encouraging early ambulation and leg exercises

B. Administering intramuscular oxytocin for uterine contractions

C. Applying cold packs to the perineal area for pain relief

Q22: Which of the following postpartum assessment findings would warrant immediate intervention by the nurse when caring for a postpartum woman?

A. Lochia rubra on the second postpartum day

B. Fundus located one centimeter above the umbilicus on the third postpartum day

C. Perineal pain and swelling on the first postpartum day

Q23: Which medication is commonly administered to manage postpartum uterine atony and prevent postpartum hemorrhage?

A. Insulin

B. Antihypertensives

C. Oxytocic

Q24 A postpartum woman who underwent a cesarean section is at risk of developing wound infections. What type of medication would be suitable for this situation? prophylaxis in this situation?

A. Analgesics (Tylenol)

B. Antimicrobials

C. Rh Immune Globulin (RhoGAM)

Q25: A postpartum woman with a history of gestational diabetes requires insulin therapy to manage her blood glucose levels. The nurse prepares to administer the insulin subcutaneously. Which site is commonly used for insulin injection during the postpartum period?

A. Deltoid muscle

B. Vastus lateralis muscle

C. Abdomen

Q26: A postpartum woman is prescribed both an antimicrobial medication and an antihypertensive medication following a cesarean section. Which potential drug interaction should the nurse closely monitor for?

A. Increased risk of postpartum infection

B. Decreased blood pressure

C. Reduced effectiveness of the antimicrobial

Q27: A postpartum woman with type 1 diabetes is prescribed insulin to manage her blood glucose levels. What key teaching point should the nurse prioritize when educating the woman about insulin administration?

A. Avoid breastfeeding while on insulin therapy.

B. Inject insulin directly into the abdominal muscles.

C. Monitor blood glucose levels regularly and adjust insulin doses accordingly.

Q28: A postpartum woman is prescribed analgesics (Tylenol) to manage mild pain after vaginal birth. Which instruction should the nurse include in the woman's discharge teaching?

A. "Avoid breastfeeding while taking Tylenol to prevent medication transfer to the baby."

B. "Take Tylenol on an empty stomach for quicker pain relief."

C. "Do not exceed the recommended dosage of Tylenol to avoid liver damage."

Q29: A postpartum woman complains of severe perineal pain and discomfort following a vaginal birth. The nurse assesses the perineum and observes significant swelling. What is the most appropriate nursing intervention to address this common problem?

A. Apply an ice pack to the perineal area to reduce swelling and pain.

B. Administer an oral analgesic medication for immediate pain relief.

C. Encourage the woman to sit for extended periods to relieve pressure on the perineum.

Q30: A postpartum woman experiences persistent constipation following childbirth. Which nursing intervention is appropriate to address this common problem?

A. Encourage the woman to increase her intake of high-fiber foods and fluids.

B. Administer a laxative without informing the healthcare provider.

C. Limit the woman's physical activity to minimize bowel movements.

Q31: A postpartum woman reports experiencing severe pain, swelling, and discomfort in the perineal area after a vaginal birth. On assessment, the nurse observes a tear in the vaginal tissues. What complication is likely present, and what intervention is appropriate for this condition?

A. Vaginal laceration; apply cold compresses to reduce swelling and promote healing.

B. Hemorrhoids; administer oral analgesics for pain relief and advise sitz baths.

C. Breast engorgement; encourage frequent breastfeeding and offer warm compresses.

Q32: A postpartum woman asks the nurse about the importance of postpartum self-care. What should the nurse include in her response?

A. "Postpartum self-care is essential for promoting healing, managing pain, and preventing infection."

B. "Postpartum selfcare is mainly focused on taking care of your baby and ensuring their wellbeing."

C. "Postpartum self-care is not necessary, as your body will naturally recover after childbirth."

Q33: A new mother asks the nurse about contraceptive options after childbirth. What should the nurse inform her about postpartum contraception?

A. "You can resume any birth control method you were using before pregnancy."

B. "For the first six months after childbirth it's advisable to refrain from using any contraceptive methods.

C. "There are various postpartum contraceptive options available including hormonal and nonhormonal methods."

Q34: What is the primary mode of heat loss when a neonate is removed from an incubator for procedures without the use of an overhead warmer?

A. Convection

B. Evaporation

C. Radiation

Q35: Which of the following is a normal finding of male genitalia in a term neonate?

A. Retractable prepuce

B. Rugate scrotum

C. Testes in the inguinal canal

Q36: During the normal breastfeeding process what is the term used to describe the proper alignment of the infant's body in relation to the mother's breast during feeding?

A. Positioning

B. Latch On

C. Suck/Swallow/Sequence

Q37: In the context of breastfeeding, what is "Latch On" referring to?

A. The baby's ability to suck and swallow milk during feeding.

B. The frequency and duration of breastfeeding sessions.

C. The baby's attachment to the breast and formation of a proper seal for feeding.

Q38: During hand expression, the mother should be encouraged to use her thumb and fingers to compress which area of the breast for effective milk expression?

A. Areola

B. Nipple

C. Upper breast tissue

Q39: A breastfeeding mother is experiencing engorgement and is having difficulty latching her baby properly. What breast care intervention can be recommended to alleviate the discomfort and assist with latch-on?

A. Use of supplementary feedings

B. Use of breastfeeding devices

C. Expressing and storing breast milk

Q40: A breastfeeding mother is returning to work and needs to store breast milk for her baby. What key point should be emphasized in teaching her about expressing and storing breast milk?

A. Ensure frequent and prolonged pumping sessions.

B. Use a manual breast pump for optimal milk expression.

C. Store expressed milk in a clean, sterile container.

Q41: A breastfeeding mother is experiencing cracked and sore nipples. What key point of nipple care should be recommended to promote healing and prevent further irritation?

A. Use of complementary feedings

B. Use of breastfeeding devices

C. Expressing and storing breast milk

Q42: A breastfeeding mother has been diagnosed with an active, untreated tuberculosis (TB) infection. What would be the reason to avoid breastfeeding in this situation?

A. Maternal complications

B. Therapeutic medications

C. Infection/Mastitis

Q43: A breastfeeding mother is experiencing severe breast engorgement with pain and swelling. What factor or condition prevents breastfeeding in this situation?

A. Nipple problems

B. Breast engorgement

C. Insufficient milk supply

Answer: B. Breast engorgement

Q44: A mother who delivered her newborn via cesarean section is experiencing postoperative complications and is unable to visit her baby in the nursery. What is the term for the separation of the mother and newborn due to the mother's health condition?

A. Neonatal isolation

B. Newborn seclusion

C. Maternal/newborn separation

Q45 A newborn is displaying signs of jaundice shortly after birth. Among the following complications, which one is marked by a higher bilirubin level in the blood resulting in a yellowish tint on the skin or eyes?

A. Hyperbilirubinemia

B. Hypoglycemia

C. Multiple Birth

Q46: A newborn is experiencing low blood sugar levels and is displaying signs of jitteriness and poor feeding. Which of the following complications is characterized by low blood glucose levels in a newborn shortly after birth?

A. Hyperbilirubinemia

B. Hypoglycemia

C. Multiple Birth

Q47: Which of the following is a normal characteristic of parents in the postpartum period?

A. Experiencing heightened anxiety about their newborn's well-being

B. Demonstrating increased interest in social activities.

C. Expressing unconditional love and attachment towards their newborn.

Q48: Which of the following is a normal infant interaction that fosters bonding and attachment between the newborn and parents?

A. Making eye contact with the infant during feeding.

B. Keeping the newborn in a separate room during sleep.

C. Using a pacifier to soothe the baby instead of direct physical contact.

Q49: Maternal role transition refers to the process through which a woman adapts to her new role as a mother. Which of the following is a characteristic feature of maternal role transition?

A. Feeling overwhelmed with the new responsibilities of motherhood.

B. Emphasizing self-care and prioritizing personal needs over the babies.

C. Experiencing immediate emotional attachment and bonding with the newborn.

Q50: How may a toddler typically respond to the arrival of a new sibling?

A. Expressing excitement and eagerness to help care for the newborn.

B. Exhibiting regressive behavior or seeking more attention from parents.

C. Showing indifference and not displaying any reaction to the newborn.

Q51: What is a potential barrier to parent/infant interactions in the immediate postpartum period, particularly if the neonate requires specialized care?

A. Convection from an overhead warmer

B. Limited availability of breastfeeding devices

C. The mother's high hemoglobin levels

Q52: What lifestyle factor can significantly affect family integration during the postpartum period?

A. Maternal hemoglobin levels

B. Frequency of prenatal check-ups

C. Socioeconomic status

Q53: How can cultural factors influence family integration in the postpartum period?

A. By affecting the mother's hemoglobin levels during pregnancy

B. By determining the type of delivery (vaginal or cesarean)

C. By influencing the roles and expectations of family members

Q54: What is an essential consideration for healthcare providers when assessing postpartum women for intimate partner violence (IPV)?

A. Screening for IPV should only be done if the woman displays physical signs of abuse.

B. Healthcare providers should avoid asking direct questions about IPV to protect the woman's privacy.

C. Assessing for IPV should be done privately and sensitively using a validated screening tool.

Q55: A family with a history of autosomal dominant inheritance has one parent who carries the defective gene. What is the chance of each of their children developing the disease?

A) 25%

B) 50%

C) 75%

Q56: A woman who has just given birth has decided to place her baby for adoption. As a nurse, what is the most appropriate action to take when discussing the adoption process with the mother?

A) Encourage her to reconsider her decision and keep the baby.

B) Provide emotional support and respect her decision without judgment.

C) Advise her to involve the baby's father in the adoption process.

Q57: A mother has recently experienced the loss of her newborn during childbirth. She is expressing feelings of sadness, guilt, and disbelief. As a nurse, what is the most appropriate action to provide support to the mother?

A) Advise her to avoid talking about her feelings to prevent further distress.

B) Offer condolences and encourage her to seek counseling or support groups.

C) Tell her that it is essential to move on from the loss and focus on the future.

Q58: A pregnant woman is reluctant to undergo a medically necessary cesarean section despite potential risks to her and the baby is health. As a nurse how would you uphold the ethical principle of autonomy?

A Inform the woman that she must undergo the procedure for the wellbeing of the baby.

B Respect the woman is right to make informed decisions about her own body and her baby is care.

C Consult with the healthcare team to override the woman's decision for the safety of the baby.

Q59: A newborn is placed under a radiant warmer immediately after birth. What is the primary purpose of using a radiant warmer for the newborn?

A) To prevent heat loss due to convection

B) To promote evaporative heat loss

C) To minimize heat loss through radiation

Q60: A preterm newborn is admitted to the neonatal intensive care unit NICU or placed in an incubator to maintain body temperature. Which heat loss mechanism is most effectively minimized by the use of an incubator?

A) Convection

B) Evaporation

C) Radiation

Q61: A term newborn is experiencing mild respiratory distress shortly after birth. Which laboratory finding is most likely to be elevated in response to this condition?

A) Hemoglobin level

B) Platelet count

C) White blood cell count

Q62: A newborn is born preterm and requires admission to the neonatal intensive care unit NICU due to respiratory distress syndrome. Which laboratory finding is expected to be low in this newborn?

A) Blood glucose level

B) Surfactant level

C) Bilirubin level

Q63: When assessing the newborn's gestational age, which characteristic is commonly used to evaluate neuromuscular maturity?

A) Ballard Score

B) Dubowitz Score

C) New Ballard Score

Q64: In the New Ballard Score, which assessment evaluates the newborn's physical maturity?

A) Posture

B) Square window

C) Skin texture

Q65: When performing the neurobehavioral assessment of a newborn, which reflex is tested by stroking the baby's cheek, causing them to turn their head and open their mouth?

A) Moro reflex

B) Babinski reflex

C) Rooting reflex

Q66: During the sensory assessment of a newborn, which response indicates a normal sense of hearing?

A) Blinking in response to bright light

B) Startling or jumping at loud noises

C) Turning the head toward a voice or sound

Q67: During a newborn's physical assessment, the nurse observes a small, bluish-green pigmented area on the lower back. What does this finding indicate?

A) Possible cardiac abnormality

B) Normal variation in the integumentary system

C) Respiratory distress syndrome

Q68: A newborn's umbilical cord stump has dried and turned brownish-black. What is the appropriate nursing intervention for cord care at this stage?

A) Apply hydrogen peroxide to the cord stump after every diaper change.

B) Keep the cord stump clean and dry, avoiding submerging the baby in water until it falls off naturally.

C) Apply an antibiotic ointment to the cord stump twice a day.

Q69: A newborn baby has not passed meconium within the first 24 hours after birth. What action should the nurse take?

A) Encourage the mother to breastfeed more frequently.

B) Administer a rectal stimulation to help the baby pass meconium.

C) Notify the healthcare provider for further evaluation.

Q70: A mother inquiries about newborn circumcision for her baby boy. What information should the nurse provide to the mother about the procedure?

A) Newborn circumcision is a routine procedure performed on all male infants shortly after birth.

B) The decision to circumcise is a personal one or it is essential for parents to weigh the benefits and risks before making a choice.

C) Circumcision is mandatory for all male infants to prevent future health issues.

Q71: A newborn is crying and showing signs of distress. What comfort measure can the nurse use to soothe the baby?

A) Offer a pacifier dipped in honey or sugar water.

B) Swaddle the baby snugly in a soft blanket.

C) Place the baby in a separate room to minimize stimulation.

Q72: A newborn is experiencing skin dryness and irritation. What comfort measure can the nurse recommend to the parents?

A) Apply petroleum jelly directly on the irritated skin.

B) Avoid bathing the baby frequently to retain natural oils.

C) Use scented baby lotions to keep the skin moisturized.

Q73: Newborn screening for critical congenital heart disease (CCHD) is performed using:

A) Chest X-ray

B) Echocardiogram

C) Pulse oximetry

Q74: The recommended time frame for performing newborn screening for critical congenital heart disease (CCHD) is:

A) Within 24 hours of birth

B) On the second day after birth

C) Before discharge from the birthing facility

Q75: Which of the following statements is true regarding newborn skin care?

A) Newborn skin is fully mature and resilient at birth.

B) The use of harsh soaps and baby wipes is recommended to cleanse the skin.

C) Lanolin-based creams are not suitable for newborn skin.

Q76: Which skin condition is common in newborns and appears as small white or yellowish bumps on the nose, chin, or cheeks?

A) Milia

B) Erythema toxic

C) Mongolian spots

Q77: To promote safe sleep for a newborn, which position should the nurse recommend for placing the baby during sleep?

A) Supine position (on the back)

B) Prone position (on the stomach)

C) Lateral position (on the side)

Q78: During tummy time, what should parents be encouraged to do?

A) Place the newborn on their back to play.

B) Provide a soft surface, such as a waterbed, for tummy time.

C) Supervise the baby while they are awake and on their tummy.

Q79: What is the purpose of administering oral sucrose to a newborn?

A) To prevent vitamin K deficiency

B) To promote breastfeeding

C) To provide pain relief during procedures

Q80: Which vitamin is routinely administered to newborns to prevent bleeding disorders?

A) Vitamin A

B) Vitamin C

C) Vitamin K

Q81: When assessing a newborn's general status at birth, which of the following signs indicates the need for immediate resuscitation?

A) Active crying and normal skin color

B) Breathing with irregular shallow respirations

C) Slow but steady heart rate above 100 beats per minute

Q82: What is the recommended initial step for newborn resuscitation?

A) Administering oxygen through a mask

B) Clearing the airway with suction

C) Providing tactile stimulation

Q83: During the initial steps of newborn resuscitation, what is the first priority for the healthcare provider?

A) Administering oxygen through a mask

B) Clearing the airway of any obstructions

C) Providing tactile stimulation

Q84: Which of the following is a critical component of the "A-B-C" approach in newborn resuscitation?

A) Assessment

B) Breathing

C) Comfort

Q85: Which medication is commonly administered to newborns to prevent hemorrhagic disease and promote blood clotting?

A) Ibuprofen

B) Vitamin K

C) Acetaminophen

Q86: Which drug is used as a first-line treatment for newborns with respiratory distress syndrome (RDS) due to surfactant deficiency?

A) Dopamine

B) Epinephrine

C) Exogenous surfactant

Q87: After providing interventions for a newborn with respiratory distress, which assessment finding indicates the effectiveness of the interventions?

A) Decreased heart rate

B) Cyanosis worsens

C) Respiratory rate remains the same

Q88: A preterm newborn receives surfactant therapy for respiratory distress. What observation suggests that the surfactant treatment is effective?

A) Decreased oxygen saturation

B) Improved lung compliance

C) Increased apnea episodes

Q89: The Apgar score is used to assess the newborn's:

A) Temperature

B) Respiratory status

C) Blood glucose level

Q90: When is the Apgar score typically assessed after birth?

A) 5 minutes

B) 10 minutes

C) 15 minutes

Q91: Postpartum hemorrhage PPH is defined as the loss of blood in excess of:

A) five hundred milliliters after vaginal birth or thousands of milliliters after cesarean birth

B) 250 milliliters after vaginal birth or 500 milliliters after cesarean birth

C) 1000 milliliters after vaginal birth or 1500 milliliters after cesarean birth

Q92: The most common cause of postpartum hemorrhage is:

A) Uterine atony

B) Retained placental fragments

C) Vaginal lacerations

Q93: Thrombophlebitis is a condition characterized by inflammation and blood clot formation in:

A) The lungs

B) The legs

C) The uterus

Q94: Which of the following is a common predisposing factor for thrombophlebitis in the postpartum period?

A) Young maternal age

B) Primiparity (first-time pregnancy)

C) Cesarean birth

Q95: The most common symptom of thrombophlebitis is:

A) Chest pain

B) Shortness of breath

C) Leg pain and swelling

Q96: Which of the following conditions is characterized by a blood clot that travels to the lungs and blocks the blood flow?

A) Deep vein thrombosis (DVT)

B) Pulmonary embolus (PE)

C) thrombophlebitis

Q97: Among postpartum women, what is the primary source of pulmonary embolism?

A) Blood clots in the legs

B) Infection in the lungs

C) Congenital heart disease

Q98: Disseminated Intravascular Coagulation (DIC) is a condition characterized by:

A) Excessive blood clotting

B) Increased platelet count

C) Impaired blood clotting and widespread bleeding

Q99: DIC is often associated with which of the following maternal conditions?

A) Gestational diabetes

B) Preeclampsia

C) Iron deficiency anemia

Q100: HELLP syndrome is a serious complication associated with:

A) Gestational diabetes

B) Preeclampsia

C) Premature rupture of membranes

Q101: The acronym "HELLP" stands for:

A) Hemolysis, Elevated Liver enzymes, Low Platelet count

B) Hypertension, Enlarged Liver, Late Pregnancy

C) High Fever, Elevated Leukocytes, Low Hemoglobin

Q102: What is a hematoma in the context of postpartum complications?

A) An infection of the uterine lining

B) A blood clot in the deep veins of the legs

C) A localized collection of blood outside blood vessels

Q103: Which type of hematoma occurs between the uterine wall and the placenta after childbirth?

A) Subchorionic hematoma

B) Subdural hematoma

C) Subinvolution hematoma

Q104: What is the most common cause of a perineal hematoma after vaginal delivery?

A) Uterine atony

B) Episiotomy

C) Placenta previa

Q105: Chronic hypertension in pregnancy is defined as:

A) New-onset hypertension during pregnancy

B) Hypertension diagnosed before pregnancy or before 20 weeks of gestation

C) Hypertension that develops after 20 weeks of gestation

Q106: Women with chronic hypertension are at increased risk of developing complications during pregnancy, including:

A) Gestational diabetes

B) Preterm labor

C) Preeclampsia

Q107: What is the goal of blood pressure management in pregnant women with chronic hypertension?

A) Keeping blood pressure consistently below 100/60 mmHg

B) Reducing blood pressure to normal levels during pregnancy Maintaining blood pressure within an acceptable range to prevent harm to the mother and fetus

Q108: Gestational hypertension is defined as:

A) Hypertension that is present before pregnancy and persists throughout gestation

B) Hypertension that develops after 20 weeks of gestation and resolves by 12 weeks postpartum

C) Hypertension that develops after 20 weeks of gestation but persists beyond 12 weeks postpartum

Q109: Gestational hypertension is characterized by elevated blood pressure readings of:

A) 120/80 mmHg or higher on two occasions, at least 4 hours apart

B) 140/90 mmHg or higher on two occasions, at least 4 hours apart

C) 160/100 mmHg or higher on two occasions, at least 4 hours apart

Q110: What is eclampsia?

A) Seizures that occur during pregnancy and in the postpartum period

B) A rare condition causing elevated blood pressure in newborns

C) A form of hypothermia in neonates

Q111: Eclampsia is most commonly associated with which of the following conditions?

A) Preeclampsia

B) Gestational diabetes

C) Placenta previa

Q112: Which postpartum complication is characterized by inflammation of the lining of the uterus?

A. Endometritis

B. Mastitis

C. Retained placenta

Q113: A postpartum mother with a fever, abdominal pain, and foul-smelling lochia should be assessed for which complication?

A. Endometritis

B. Thrombophlebitis

C. Preeclampsia

Q114: A postpartum woman who had a cesarean section is at risk for which type of infection?

A. Urinary tract infection

B. Wound infection

C. Respiratory infection

Q115: Which of the following is a common symptom of wound infection in the postpartum period?

A. Vaginal bleeding

B. Abdominal cramps

C. Redness, swelling, and warmth at the incision site

Q116: The most appropriate nursing intervention to prevent wound infection in the postpartum woman is:

A. Applying warm compresses to the incision site

B. Administering prophylactic antibiotics

C. Encouraging ambulation and deep breathing exercises

Q117: A postpartum woman presents with fever, chills, and pain in the lower abdomen. Upon assessment, the nurse observes redness and warmth over the affected area. Which postpartum complication should the nurse suspect?

A. Endometritis

B. Urinary tract infection

C. Septic pelvic thrombophlebitis

Q118: Septic pelvic thrombophlebitis is most commonly associated with which type of delivery?

A. Vaginal delivery

B. Cesarean section

C. Vacuum-assisted delivery

Q119: Which of the following's a risk factor for the development of septic pelvic thrombophlebitis?

A. Maternal age above 35 years

B. History of blood clotting disorders

C. Primiparity (first-time pregnancy)

Q120: A postpartum woman complains of frequent urination and a burning sensation during voiding. Which postpartum complication should the nurse suspect?

A. Mastitis

B. Urinary tract infection

C. Endometritis

Q121: Which of the following is a common causative organism for urinary tract infections in postpartum women?

A. Escherichia coli (E. coli)

B. Group B Streptococcus (GBS)

C. Staphylococcus aureus

Q122: The nurse is teaching a postpartum woman about measures to prevent urinary tract infections. Which instruction should the nurse include?

A. "Limit your fluid intake to reduce the frequency of urination."

B. "Empty your bladder regularly and completely, especially after childbirth."

C. "Avoid washing the perineal area to prevent irritation."

Q123: A postpartum woman with a history of gestational diabetes is at risk for which postpartum complication?

A. Preeclampsia

B. Endometritis

C. Postpartum diabetes

Q124: What is the main worry for a woman with gestational diabetes right after childbirth?

A. Developing hypoglycemia

B. Managing labor pain

C. Controlling postpartum hemorrhage

Q125: A postpartum woman reports having difficulty falling asleep and frequently waking up during the night. Which sleep disturbance is commonly experienced during the postpartum period?

A. Sleep apnea

B. Insomnia

C. Narcolepsy

Q126: What is a common contributing factor to sleep disturbances in the postpartum period?

A. High levels of estrogen or progesterone

B. Frequent breastfeeding during the night

C. Decreased physical activity

Q127: The nurse is providing education to a postpartum woman about improving sleep quality. Which recommendation should the nurse give to the woman?

A. Drink caffeinated beverages in the evening to stay awake during nighttime feedings.

B. Sleep when the baby sleeps during the day to make up for nighttime awakenings.

C. Engage in vigorous exercise close to bedtime to promote better sleep.

Q128: A postpartum woman is experiencing persistent feelings of sadness, loss of interest, and difficulty bonding with her newborn. Which postpartum mood disorder should the nurse suspect?

A. Postpartum depression

B. Postpartum psychosis

C. Postpartum anxiety disorder

Q129: What is a common risk factor for developing postpartum depression?

A. Primiparity (first-time pregnancy)

B. Young maternal age

C. History of multiple gestations

Q130: A postpartum woman presents with hallucinations, delusions, and disorganized behavior. Which postpartum mood disorder should the nurse suspect?

A. Postpartum depression

B. Postpartum psychosis

C. Postpartum anxiety disorder

Q131: A postpartum woman is exhibiting signs of substance abuse, such as altered mental status and slurred speech. Which substance should the nurse suspect as the likely cause of these symptoms?

A. Marijuana

B. Heroin

C. Alcohol

Q132: What is the most critical concern for a postpartum woman who is abusing substances during the breastfeeding period?

A. Decreased milk production

B. Neonatal withdrawal symptoms

C. Risk of transmitting substances to the baby through breast milk

Answer: C. Risk of transmitting substances to the baby through breast milk

Q133: A newborn is born with cyanosis, tachypnea (rapid breathing), and a heart murmur. Which condition should the nurse suspect in this newborn?

A. Patent ductus arteriosus (PDA)

B. Tetralogy of Fallot (TOF)

C. Atrial septal defect (ASD)

Q134: A newborn presents with cyanosis, tachypnea, and clubbing of the fingers and toes. Which congenital heart defect is most likely responsible for these findings?

A. Ventricular septal defect (VSD)

B. Tetralogy of Fallot (TOF)

C. Atrial septal defect (ASD)

Q135: Which of the following is a common clinical manifestation of cyanotic heart disease in newborns?

A. Hyperoxia and decreased respiratory rate

B. Pallor and bradycardia

C. Cyanosis that worsens with crying or agitation

Q136: A newborn is diagnosed with a cyanotic heart disease characterized by an opening between the atria, allowing blood to mix. Which condition is most likely responsible for this presentation?

A. Patent ductus arteriosus (PDA)

B. Ventricular septal defect (VSD)

C. Tetralogy of Fallot (TOF)

Q137: Apnea is a common condition in preterm infants and can lead to serious complications. Which of the following is NOT a predisposing factor for apnea in newborns?

A. Prematurity

B. Maternal smoking during pregnancy

C. Increased body weight

Q138: Transient Tachypnea of the Newborn (TTN) is a common respiratory condition that affects neonates shortly after birth. Which of the following best describes the pathophysiology of TTN?

A. Accumulation of excess surfactant in the alveoli

B. Delayed closure of the ductus arteriosus

C. Retained lung fluid causing respiratory distress

Q139: Pneumothorax is a potentially serious respiratory condition that can affect newborns. Can you explain the pathophysiology of pneumothorax in a neonate in simpler terms?

A. Accumulation of excess surfactant in the alveoli

B. Infection of the lung tissue by bacteria or viruses

C. Accumulation of air in the pleural space, causing lung collapse

Q140: Meconium aspiration syndrome is a serious respiratory condition that can affect newborns. What is the most common route of meconium aspiration by the neonate?

A. Inhalation of meconium-stained amniotic fluid during labor or delivery

B. Ingestion of meconium after birth while breastfeeding

C. Meconium absorption through the skin during the postnatal period

Q141: A neonate is experiencing abnormal, uncontrolled electrical activity in the brain, leading to sudden jerking movements and altered consciousness. Which of the following terms best describes this condition?

A. Hypoxia

B. Seizures

C. Cyanosis

Q142: A newborn is exhibiting tremors shortly after birth. These tremors are fine, rapid, and involve the entire body. The mother is concerned about the baby's well-being. What is the most appropriate response by the nurse?

A. "These tremors are concerning and may indicate a neurological problem. I will notify the doctor immediately."

B. "These tremors are normal and may be related to the baby's immature nervous system. We will continue to monitor the baby is condition."

C. "These tremors are caused by low blood sugar levels in the baby. We will administer glucose to resolve the issue."

Q143: A full-term newborn presents with signs of increased intracranial pressure, including bulging fontanelle, irritability, and high-pitched cry. The nurse suspects an intracranial hemorrhage. Which of the following is the most appropriate action?

A. Administer antipyretics to reduce fever.

B. Perform a lumbar puncture to confirm the diagnosis.

C. Notify the healthcare provider immediately for further evaluation and intervention.

Q144: A newborn is diagnosed with a neural tube defect (NTD). Which of the following interventions should the nurse prioritize?

A. Administering antibiotics to prevent infection.

B. Placing the newborn in a prone position to reduce pressure on the spine.

C. Initiating immediate surgical repair of the defect.

Q145 A newborn is admitted to the neonatal intensive care unit NICU exhibiting symptoms of withdrawal from a substance abused during pregnancy. What substance is often linked to neonatal withdrawal syndrome?

A. Caffeine

B. Nicotine

C. Folic acid

Q146: A newborn is born with a suspected gastrointestinal anomaly. The nurse assesses the baby for abdominal distension, vomiting, and failure to pass meconium. These clinical manifestations are consistent with which gastrointestinal condition?

A. Intussusception

B. Hirschsprung's disease

C. Pyloric stenosis

Q147: A neonate presents with bilious vomiting, abdominal distension, and "double bubble" sign on abdominal X-ray. What condition is the newborn likely experiencing?

A. Intussusception

B. Hirschsprung's disease

C. Duodenal atresia

Q148 A newborns admitted to the neonatal intensive care unit NICU with pallor tachycardia or lethargy. The nurse suspects the neonate may have anemia. Which diagnostic test would be most appropriate to confirm this suspicion?

A. Blood glucose level

B. Serum bilirubin level

C. Complete blood count (CBC) with hemoglobin level

Q149: A newborn is at risk for vitamin K deficiency, which can lead to bleeding disorders. Which intervention is essential to prevent vitamin K deficiency bleeding in the neonate?

A. Delayed cord clamping

B. Administration of vitamin K injection

C. Exclusive breastfeeding without supplementation

Q150: A mother refuses to have her newborn receive a vitamin K injection due to personal beliefs. The nurse educates the mother about the potential consequences of vitamin K deficiency in newborns. What complication is of utmost concern in these infants?

A. Respiratory distress syndrome

B. Hyperbilirubinemia

C. Intracranial hemorrhage

Q151 A term newborn is admitted with jaundice. Upon assessment, the nurse notices that the newborn's sclera and skin have a yellowish tinge. The nurse suspects hyperbilirubinemia in the infant What frequently causes hyperbilirubinemia in the first few days after birth?

A. Physiologic jaundice

B. Inadequate iron intake

C. Congenital heart defect

Q152: A newborn is born with ABO incompatibility due to the mother's blood type being O and the baby's blood type being A. Which of the following reactions is commonly seen in this condition?

A. Hemolytic disease of the newborn (HDN)

B. Hypoglycemia

C. Respiratory distress syndrome RDS

Q153: A pregnant woman with blood type O has given birth to a baby with blood type AB. What is the risk of ABO incompatibility in this situation?

A. Low risk

B. Moderate risk

C. High risk

Q154: Hemolytic disease of the newborn (HDN) occurs when there is a Rh incompatibility between the mother and the baby. Which of the following blood types in the mother can cause HDN in the baby if the baby's blood type is Rh-positive?

A. Blood type O

B. Blood type A

C. Blood type B

Q155: G6PD deficiency is an inherited disorder that affects the red blood cells. Which of the following substances or conditions can trigger a hemolytic crisis in a neonate with G6PD deficiency?

A. Exposure to sunlight

B. Breastfeeding during the first twenty-four hours of life

C. Administration of vitamin K injection

Q156: A neonate is diagnosed with G6PD deficiency. The healthcare provider advises the mother to avoid certain foods to prevent a hemolytic crisis in the baby. Which of the following foods should be avoided in a neonate with G6PD deficiency?

A. Fruits rich in vitamin C

B. Dairy products

C. Legumes and beans

Q157: Polycythemia is a condition in which there is an increased number of red blood cells in the neonate is circulation. Which of the following signs and symptoms is commonly associated with polycythemia in a newborn?

A. Cyanosis and labored breathing

B. Jaundice and dark-colored urine

C. Pallor and lethargy

Q158 One of the possibility factors for the development of polycythemia in the neonate is maternal diabetes. Which of the following mechanisms contributes to the increased possibility of polycythemia in infants of diabetic mothers?

A. Fetal hypoglycemia leading to increased red blood cell production

B. Impaired transfer of oxygen across the placenta

C. Maternal hyperglycemia causing an increase in fetal blood volume

Q159: Hyper viscosity is a condition characterized by an increased thickness of the blood due to excessive red blood cells or other components. Which of the following neonatal conditions can lead to hyper viscosity?

A. Polycythemia

B. Anemia

C. Physiologic jaundice

Q160: A neonate's diagnosed with thrombocytopenia. Which of the following interventions should the maternal nurse prioritize to prevent bleeding complications in the newborn?

A. Administering vitamin K injection

B. Initiating phototherapy for jaundice

C. Minimizing heel sticks and venipunctures

Q161: A neonate is exhibiting signs of sepsis, and a blood culture is ordered to confirm the diagnosis. Which of the following interventions should the maternal nurse prioritize while awaiting the culture results?

A. Initiating antibiotic therapy

B. Administering antipyretics

C. Providing phototherapy for jaundice

Q162: A newborn is suspected to have a bacterial infection. Which laboratory test should the maternal nurse prioritize to assess the baby's response to the infection and identify potential complications?

A. Blood Culture

B. Liver Function Test (LFT)

C. Electrolyte Panel

Q163: A neonate is born to a mother with Group B Streptococcus (GBS) colonization. Which component of the complete blood count (CBC) and differential is essential to monitor in the newborn to detect early signs of infection?

A. Hemoglobin (Hb) level

B. White Blood Cell (WBC) count

C. Platelet count

Q164: A neonate is suspected of having meningitis. Which diagnostic procedure should the maternal nurse anticipate to confirm the diagnosis and assess for central nervous system infection?

A. Ultrasound of the brain

B. Lumbar Puncture (LP)

C. X-ray of the skull

Q165: A term newborn presents with signs of increased intracranial pressure. The healthcare provider orders a lumbar puncture to assess for suspected infection. Before the procedure, what action should the maternal nurse prioritize?

A. Administer intravenous antibiotics

B. Obtain informed consent from the parents

C. Monitor the newborn's vital signs continuously

Q166: A newborn is showing signs of respiratory distress, including coughing wheezing or tachypnea. The maternal nurse suspects a viral respiratory infection. Which virus is most likely responsible for these symptoms?

A. Influenza virus

B. Respiratory syncytial virus RSV

C. Cytomegalovirus (CMV)

Q167: A newborn is born with conjunctivitis and a purulent discharge from the eyes. The maternal nurse suspects a sexually transmitted infection (STI) acquired during childbirth. Which STI is most likely responsible for these symptoms?

A. Chlamydia trachomatis

B. Herpes simplex virus (HSV)

C. Human papillomavirus (HPV)

Q168: A neonate presents with skin vesicles and ulcers on the mouth, palms, and soles. The maternal nurse suspects a sexually transmitted infection transmitted from the mother during birth. Which STI is the likely cause of these findings?

A. Gonorrhea

B. Syphilis

C. The human immunodeficiency virus HIV

Q169: A neonate born with a suspected bacterial infection is prescribed an intravenous antibiotic. The maternal nurse is teaching the parents about the medication. Which statement by the parents indicates a need for further education?

A. "We will monitor for any signs of an allergic reaction like rash or difficulty breathing."

B. "We'll make sure to give the antibiotic on an empty stomach to enhance its absorption."

C. "If we notice any side effects, we'll inform the healthcare provider promptly."

Q170: A newborn is diagnosed with a suspected viral infection, and the healthcare provider prescribes an antiviral medication. What is the primary goal of using antiviral drugs in the neonate?

A. To reduce fever and inflammation

B. To eradicate the viral infection completely

C. To inhibit viral replication and reduce severity of symptoms

Q171: A neonate is born with a genetic condition that impairs the production of certain enzymes involved in glucose metabolism. As a result, the neonate is at possibility of developing hypoglycemia shortly after birth. Which of the following is the most appropriate nursing intervention to prevent hypoglycemia in this newborn?

A. Administering a bolus of intravenous glucose solution

B. Encouraging early and frequent breastfeeding

C. Placing the neonate in a radiant warmer

Q172: A neonate is born with an inborn error of metabolism that affects the breakdown of certain amino acids. As a result, the neonate is at possibility of developing a condition called "metabolic acidosis." Which of the following signs and symptoms would the nurse expect to observe in this neonate?

A. Rapid and deep respirations

B. Cyanosis of the lips and extremities

C. Elevated blood pressure

Q173: A couple is planning to have a child, and they both have a family history of cystic fibrosis CF. They want to know the chances of their child inheriting the disease. What's the pattern of inheritance for cystic fibrosis?

A. Autosomal dominant

B. X-linked recessive

C. Autosomal recessive

Q174: A newborn is born to a mother with poorly controlled diabetes mellitus during pregnancy. The baby is at risk for certain complications due to maternal hyperglycemia. Which of the following complications is commonly associated with infants born to diabetic mothers?

A. Hypothermia

B. Hypoglycemia

C. Hypernatremia

Q175: A newborn is being monitored in the neonatal intensive care unit NICU due to risk factors for hypoglycemia. Which of the following conditions in the newborn increases the risk of hypoglycemia?

A. Hyperinsulinemia

B. Elevated thyroid hormone levels

C. Increased cortisol production

Test 5 Answer Key

1	C	27	C	53	C
2	C	28	C	54	C
3	C	29	A	55	C
4	C	30	A	56	B
5	A	31	A	57	B
6	C	32	A	58	B
7	C	33	C	59	A
8	C	34	A	60	A
9	B	35	B	61	C
10	A	36	A	62	B
11	B	37	C	63	B
12	A	38	A	64	C
13	B	39	B	65	C
14	B	40	C	66	C
15	C	41	C	67	B
16	B	42	C	68	B
17	B	43	B	69	C
18	C	44	C	70	B
19	C	45	A	71	B
20	A	46	B	72	B
21	A	47	C	73	C
22	B	48	A	74	C
23	C	49	C	75	C
24	B	50	B	76	A
25	C	51	A	77	A
26	C	52	C	78	C

79	C	106	C	133	B
80	C	107	C	134	B
81	B	108	B	135	C
82	C	109	B	136	B
83	B	110	A	137	C
84	B	111	A	138	C
85	B	112	A	139	C
86	C	113	A	140	A
87	A	114	B	141	B
88	B	115	C	142	B
89	B	116	B	143	C
90	A	117	C	144	C
91	A	118	B	145	B
92	A	119	B	146	B
93	B	120	B	147	C
94	C	121	A	148	C
95	C	122	B	149	B
96	B	123	C	150	C
97	A	124	A	151	A
98	C	125	B	152	A
99	B	126	B	153	C
100	B	127	B	154	A
101	A	128	A	155	A
102	C	129	B	156	C
103	A	130	B	157	A
104	B	131	C	158	C
105	B	132	B	159	A

160	C	166	B	172	A
161	A	167	A	173	C
162	A	168	B	174	B
163	B	169	B	175	A
164	B	170	C		
165	B	171	B		

Maternal Newborn Nursing Exam Practice Test 6

Q 1: A pregnant woman's experiencing vaginal bleeding during the second trimester. Is there something that could be worrisome or concerning?

A. Implantation bleeding

B. Braxton Hicks contractions

C. Placenta previa

Q 2: A 36-year old pregnant woman presents to the clinic for a routine antenatal checkup. The nurse informs her about a recommended prenatal screening test for maternal age-related concerns. What screening test is typically offered to pregnant women of advanced maternal age to assess fetal chromosomal abnormalities?

A. Non-stress test (NST)

B. Group B Streptococcus (GBS) screening

C. Amniocentesis

Q 3: A pregnant woman with gestational diabetes mellitus GDM is seeking advice on managing her condition through diet. Which dietary approach is most appropriate for managing blood glucose levels in women with GDM?

A. High-carbohydrate diet

B. Low-fat diet

C. Balanced diet with controlled carbohydrate intake

Q4: During an antenatal check-up, a pregnant woman mentions a previous pregnancy with preeclampsia. What potential obstetrical history factor should the nurse consider, which could increase the risk of developing preeclampsia again in this pregnancy?

A. History of multiple gestations

B. History of a large-for-gestational-age baby

C. History of chronic hypertension

Q5: A pregnant woman from a different cultural background expresses concerns about receiving prenatal care in a new country. What psychosocial/cultural issue should the nurse consider to ensure effective communication and promote trust between the woman and the healthcare team?

A. Language barriers and interpreter services

B. Traditional birthing practices and rituals

C. Differences in maternal clothing preferences

Q6: A couple is seeking fertility treatments to conceive, and the healthcare provider recommends in vitro fertilization (IVF). What antenatal consideration should be discussed with the couple before proceeding with IVF?

A. The risk of preterm labor and delivery

B. Potential for multiple gestations

C. Importance of prenatal vitamin supplementation

Q7: A pregnant woman in her second trimester is concerned about experiencing shortness of breath. What physiological change associated with pregnancy contributes to the sensation of increased breathlessness during this period?

A. Increased tidal volume

B. Decreased respiratory rate

C. Increased lung capacity

Q8: During an antenatal assessment, a pregnant woman reports frequent headaches and visual disturbances. Which antepartum complication is characterized by these symptoms and requires immediate medical attention?

A. Gestational diabetes mellitus (GDM)

B. Preterm labor

C. Preeclampsia

Q9: A pregnant woman with a history of a previous preterm birth is at possibility of another preterm delivery in her current pregnancy. What antepartum intervention is beneficial in reducing the risk of preterm birth in this woman?

A. Continuous electronic fetal monitoring during labor

B. Cervical cerclage placement

C. Induction of labor at 39 weeks gestation

Q10: A pregnant woman at 28 weeks of gestation is undergoing a biophysical profile (BPP) to assess fetal well-being. Which of the following parameters is included in the BPP assessment?

A. Fetal heart rate pattern

B. Maternal blood glucose levels

C. Fetal karyotyping

Q11: A pregnant woman with a history of obesity is at risk of developing a common complication related to her weight. What antenatal condition is she more likely to experience due to obesity?

A. Gestational diabetes mellitus (GDM)

B. Eclampsia

C. Placenta previa

Answer

Q12: A pregnant woman in active labor is experiencing variable decelerations in the fetal heart rate pattern. What is the primary cause of variable decelerations, and how should the nurse respond?

A. Variable decelerations are caused by cord compression, and the nurse should change the mother's position, administer oxygen, and prepare for potential emergency interventions.

B. Variable decelerations are a normal finding during active labor, and no intervention is required.

C. Variable decelerations are caused by fetal head compression, and the nurse should encourage the mother to push during contractions.

Maternal Postpartum Assessment, Management, and Education

Q13: During the postpartum period, it is important to assess the perineum for any signs of trauma or injury. Which maternal position is recommended for assessing the perineum?

A. Supine position with legs elevated

B. Lateral position with knees bent

C. Lithotomy position with legs in stirrups

Q14: A postpartum woman complains of shortness of breath and chest pain. Which condition should the nurse suspect and take immediate action?

A. Pulmonary embolism

B. Atelectasis

C. Pneumonia

Q15: During the postpartum period, a woman's blood pressure is monitored closely. Which of the following blood pressure readings should the nurse consider normal?

A. 140/90 mmHg

B. 120/80 mmHg

C. 110/70 mmHg

Q16: During a postpartum assessment, a nurse notices that a woman's lochia has a foul-smelling odor and is accompanied by fever and uterine tenderness. Which of the following conditions should the nurse suspect?

A. Postpartum hemorrhage

B. Endometritis

C. Mastitis

Q17: A postpartum woman is experiencing hemorrhoids, which are causing discomfort and pain. Which of the following measures should the nurse recommend to manage hemorrhoids during the postpartum period?

A. Applying cold packs to the perineum

B. Avoiding the use of pain medication

C. Sits baths with warm water

Q18: During the postpartum period, many women experience physiological changes in their gastrointestinal system. Which of the following gastrointestinal changes is a common occurrence after childbirth?

A. Increased gastric acidity

B. Decreased appetite

C. Slowed bowel motility

Q19: A postpartum woman with a history of thrombocytopenia presents with excessive bleeding and prolonged clotting time after childbirth What condition is most likely responsible for her symptoms?

A. Disseminated intravascular coagulation DIC

B. Hemolytic disease of the newborn (HDN)

C. Gestational hypertension

Q20: Which hormone is responsible for stimulating uterine contractions during childbirth and is also involved in the milk ejection reflex during breastfeeding?

A. Oxytocin

B. Prolactin

C. Estrogen

Q21: During postpartum education, the nurse informs the new mother about the importance of perineal care to prevent infection and promote healing. Which of the following instructions should the nurse include in the teaching?

A. Use warm water to cleanse the perineal area after each voiding or bowel movement.

B. Pat the perineal area dry with a clean towel after cleansing.

C. Apply hydrogen peroxide to the perineal area to disinfect the wound.

Q22: During the comprehensive postpartum health assessment, the nurse notes that the fundus of a postpartum woman is firm, at the level of the umbilicus, and deviated to the right side. What action should the nurse take based on this finding?

A. Document the findings as a normal postpartum variation.

B. Assist the woman in emptying her bladder to reposition the fundus.

C. Perform a gentle fundal massage to promote involution.

Q23: Which medications commonly used in the postpartum period to help control hypertension in women with preeclampsia?

A. Antiretroviral

B. Diuretics

C. Antihypertensives

Q24: A breastfeeding mother with anemia may require iron supplementation. How much elemental iron is typically recommended daily for pregnant and lactating women with normal hemoglobin levels?

A. 30 mg of elemental iron

B. 60 mg of elemental iron

C. 120 mg of elemental iron

Q25: A laboring woman requests pain relief after a vaginal birth. The nurse plans to administer an analgesic medication. Which analgesic is frequently used in the postpartum period to provide pain relief without interfering with breastfeeding?

A. Morphine

B. Ibuprofen

C. Fentanyl

Q26: A lactating woman who underwent a tubal ligation is prescribed an oral contraceptive to prevent future pregnancies. Which medication interaction should the nurse discuss with the woman?

A. Increased risk of breast engorgement

B. Decreased effectiveness of the oral contraceptive

C. Enhanced milk production

Q27: A new mother is prescribed antimicrobial medication after a cesarean section. What essential information should the nurse include in the woman's medication education?

A. "Antimicrobials may cause drowsiness, so avoid driving or operating heavy machinery."

B. "Take the antimicrobial medication with a small glass of grapefruit juice to enhance absorption."

C. ""Complete the full course of antimicrobial therapy even if you start feeling better. "."

Q28: A postpartum women prescribed an antihypertensive medication to manage her blood pressure after being diagnosed with preeclampsia. What important information should the nurse include in the woman's teaching plan regarding this medication?

A. "You should discontinue the medication once your blood pressure returns to normal."

B. "Monitor your blood pressure daily and adjust the dosage accordingly based on the readings."

C. ""Change positions slowly, especially when standing up, to minimize dizziness."

Q29: A new mother reports feeling significant discomfort due to engorgement of her breasts. What nursing intervention is appropriate to manage this common problem?

A. Encourage the mother to breastfeed frequently on demand.

B. Apply cold cabbage leaves to the breasts for relief.

C. Advise the mother to avoid breastfeeding until the engorgement subsides.

Q30: A postpartum woman is experiencing pain and irritation due to hemorrhoids. Which nursing intervention is appropriate to address this common problem?

A. Apply a warm compress to the affected area for pain relief.

B. Administer a nonsteroidal anti-inflammatory drug NSAID for pain management.

C. Advise the woman to avoid sitting for extended periods.

Q31: A postpartum woman experiences urinary retention and complains of bladder fullness and discomfort. What complication should the nurse suspect, and what intervention is appropriate?

A. Breast engorgement; encourage breastfeeding on demand and apply warm compresses.

B. Bladder distention & urinary retention; assist the woman to the bathroom and provide privacy for voiding.

C. Afterpains; administer analgesics as prescribed for pain relief.

Q32: A postpartum woman asks the nurse about the importance of nutrition during this period. How should the nurse respond?

A. "Nutrition is not very important during the postpartum period as your body has already recovered from childbirth."

B. "Maintaining a balanced and nutritious diet's crucial during the postpartum period to support your recovery and breastfeeding."

C. "You should focus on restricting your calorie intake during the postpartum period to aid in weight loss."

Q33: A postpartum woman expresses concerns about breastfeeding while using a contraceptive method. What should the nurse advise her regarding breastfeeding and contraception?

A. "You should avoid breastfeeding if you choose to use contraceptive methods to prevent any potential risks to your baby."

B. There are contraceptive methods safe for breastfeeding, but it's basic. to talk with your healthcare

C. "Breastfeeding provides natural contraception, and you don't need to use any additional methods."

Q34: A preeclamptic woman in the immediate postpartum period should be closely monitored for elevated blood pressure and the risk of which complication?

A. Adult respiratory distress syndrome

B. Onset of seizures (eclampsia)

C. Subdural hematoma

Q35: What is a predisposing factor for assisted delivery (forceps or vacuum) during childbirth?

A. Adolescent pregnancy

B. Multiparity (having multiple pregnancies)

C. Postdates gestation (prolonged pregnancy beyond the due date)

Q36: Which aspect of the normal breastfeeding process refers to the rhythmic pattern of the baby's mouth movements during feeding?

A. Positioning

B. Latch On

C. Suck/Swallow/Sequence

Q37: What is the term used to describe the frequency and duration of breastfeeding sessions for a newborn baby?

A. Positioning

B. Latch On

C. Timing (Frequency and Duration)

Q38: What should be the primary focus of education when teaching a breastfeeding mother about hand expression?

A. Frequency and duration of breastfeeding sessions.

B. Proper attachment of the baby to the breast.

C. Techniques for expressing milk by hand.

Q39: A breastfeeding mother is experiencing nipple soreness and pain. Which breast care intervention is most appropriate to address this issue?

A. Use of supplementary feedings

B. Use of breastfeeding devices

C. Expressing and storing breast milk

Q40: A breastfeeding mother is having difficulties with milk flow and let-down reflex. What breast care intervention can help stimulate milk ejection and improve milk flow?

A. Use of supplementary feedings

B. Use of breastfeeding devices

C. Expressing and storing breast milk

Q41: A breastfeeding mother is having difficulty with latch-on, and her baby is not effectively breastfeeding. What nipple care intervention can be recommended to assist with latch and feeding?

A. Use of complementary feedings

B. Use of breastfeeding devices

C. Expressing and storing breast milk

Q42: A breastfeeding mother has been prescribed a medication that is known to pass into breast milk and may be harmful to the infant. What prevents breastfeeding in this situation?

B. Therapeutic medications

C. Maternal complications

Q43: A breastfeeding mother has been diagnosed with human immunodeficiency virus (HIV). What prevents breastfeeding in this situation?

A. Infection/Mastitis

B. Maternal complications

C. Perinatal substance abuse

Q44: A mother is requesting to have her newborn stay with her in the room instead of being kept in the hospital nursery. What is the practice called when the newborn is kept in the same room as the mother to promote bonding and breastfeeding?

A. Rooming-in

B. Mother-infant cohabitation

C. Postnatal togetherness

Q45: A woman has given birth to twins. What is the term used to describe the situation where a mother delivers more than one baby in a single birth event?

A. Hyperbilirubinemia

B. Hypoglycemia

C. Multiple Birth

Q46: A newborn is having difficulty regulating body temperature and is at risk of heat loss. Which of the following methods of heat loss occurs when a neonate is removed from an incubator for procedures without the use of an overhead warmer?

A. Convection

B. Evaporation

C. Radiation

Q47: How does the maternal basal metabolic rate BMR change during the postpartum period?

A. It decreases gradually over the first few weeks.

B. It remains stable compared to the prenatal period.

C. It increases initially and then gradually returns to pre-pregnancy levels.

Q48: How can healthcare professionals support normal infant interactions in the postpartum period?

A. Encouraging parents to limit physical contact with the newborn to prevent overstimulation.

B. Advising parents to avoid holding the baby too often to promote independence.

C. Educating parents about the benefits of skin-to-skin contact and responsive caregiving.

Q49: During the postpartum period, healthcare providers play a crucial role in supporting maternal role transition. Which intervention can facilitate this process effectively?

A. Encouraging the mother to avoid holding the baby too often to prevent attachment issues.

B. Providing education about infant care and emotional changes during the postpartum period.

C. Advising the mother to prioritize household chores over spending time with the baby.

Q50: When discussing the introduction of a new sibling to a preschool-age child, which approach is recommended?

A. Avoid discussing the new sibling until the baby is born to prevent jealousy.

B. Present the idea of a new sibling as a surprise to make it more exciting.

C. Involve the child in discussions and preparations for the baby's arrival.

Q51: Which factor is associated with an increased risk of altered parent/infant interactions?

A. Mothers with normal hemoglobin levels

B. First-time mothers (primiparity)

C. Neonates with inguinal canal testes

Q52: How can healthcare providers promote family integration in the postpartum period?

A. Encouraging the mother to avoid skin to skin contact with the newborn.

B. Recommending limiting the time spent on each breastfeeding session.

C. Encouraging the involvement of both parents in newborn care.

Q53: What is an essential approach for healthcare providers to promote cultural sensitivity and family integration?

A. Encouraging the use of breastfeeding devices for all new mothers

B. Providing standardized postpartum care regardless of cultural background

C. Understanding and respecting cultural practices and beliefs

Q54: How can healthcare providers support postpartum women experiencing intimate partner violence?

A. Encouraging the woman to leave the abusive partner immediately.

B. Providing resources and information about community support services.

C. Advising the woman to keep the abuse confidential and not seek help.

Q55: A family with multiple children recently welcomed a new baby into their home. The older siblings seem to be having difficulty adjusting to the changes and display regressive behaviors. What is the most appropriate nursing response?

A) Advise the parents to reprimand the older siblings for regressive behaviors.

B) Acknowledge the siblings' feelings and offer reassurance and support.

C) Suggest limiting the older siblings' access to the new baby to avoid jealousy.

Q56: A mother who is planning to place her baby for adoption expresses concerns about the baby's future well-being. How can the nurse address her concerns effectively?

A) Assure her that the adopting parents will provide everything the baby needs.

B) Offer resources and information about the adoption process and support services.

C) Advise her to focus on her decision and not worry about the baby's future.

Q57: A father who has lost his newborn is experiencing intense grief and anger. How can the nurse provide support to the father during this period of perinatal grief?

A) Suggest he distract himself from the grief by engaging in work or hobbies.

B) Offer a sympathetic ear and allow him to express his feelings without judgment.

C) Advise him to avoid discussing his grief to prevent further distress.

Q58: A postpartum woman is experiencing severe pain, and the healthcare provider has prescribed opioids for pain management. How can we ensure the ethical principle of doing no harm (nonmaleficence) is applied in this situation?

A) Encourage the woman to tolerate the pain without medication to prevent potential side effects.

B) Administer the prescribed opioids while closely monitoring for any adverse effects.

C) Withhold pain relief to avoid any potential harm from medication.

Q59: A nurse is performing a newborn assessment and observes that the newborn's scrotum appears enlarged and swollen. What is the appropriate interpretation of this finding?

A) It indicates a possible inguinal hernia that requires immediate intervention.

B) It is a normal finding in a term male neonate due to maternal hormone effects.

C) It suggests an undescended testicle, requiring further evaluation.

Q60: A term newborn is born with the scrotum looking enlarged and dark in color. What's the appropriate action for the nurse to take based on this finding?

A) Notify the healthcare provider immediately as it may indicate a serious medical condition.

B) Reassure the parents that this is a normal finding in a male newborn and will resolve within a few days.

C) Administer vitamin K injection to prevent potential bleeding in the newborn's scrotum.

Q61: A full-term newborn presents with yellowish discoloration of the skin on the second day after birth. Which laboratory finding is likely to be elevated in this newborn?

A) C-reactive protein (CRP) level

B) Hemoglobin level

C) Total bilirubin level

Q62: A newborn is diagnosed with hypoglycemia shortly after birth. Which laboratory test is used to confirm and monitor the newborn's blood glucose levels?

A) Complete blood count (CBC)

B) Blood gas analysis

C) Blood glucose measurement

Q63: In the assessment of gestational age using the Dubowitz Score, what does the "square window" assessment evaluate?

A) Skin texture

B) Range of motion in the wrist

C) Degree of flexion at the knee joint

Q64: Which assessment in the Ballard Score evaluates the newborn's external ear characteristics to determine gestational age?

A) Arm recoil

B) Ear form

C) Scarf sign

Q65: When assessing the neurobehavioral responses of a newborn, which reflex is tested by supporting the baby's head in a semi-upright position and then quickly lowering them backward?

A) Moro reflex

B) Tonic neck reflex

C) Palmar grasp reflex

Q66: What is the expected response when performing the stepping reflex during the neurobehavioral assessment of a newborn?

A) The newborn will extend their arms and legs in response to being held upright with their feet touching a surface.

B) The newborn will display a crawling-like motion when placed on their abdomen.

C) The newborn will exhibit a strong grasp when an object is placed in their palm.

Q67: While performing the systems review of a newborn, the nurse auscultates a continuous machinery-like heart murmur. Which system is most likely affected?

A) Cardiac system

B) Respiratory system

C) Gastrointestinal system

Q68: A new mother asks the nurse about caring for her newborn's umbilical cord. What instruction should the nurse provide regarding the timing of cord stump separation?

A) The cord usually separates within 24 hours after birth.

B) The cord typically separates within 1 to 2 weeks after birth.

C) The cord usually separates within 4 to 6 weeks after birth.

Q69: A 2-day-old newborn is observed to have frequent urination, with clear, pale-yellow urine. The baby is breastfeeding well. What is the appropriate nursing response to the parents' concern about the baby's urination pattern?

A) Inform the parents that frequent urination is a normal finding in newborns who are breastfeeding effectively.

B) Recommend limiting the baby's fluid intake to reduce the number of urinations.

C) Advise the parents to consult a pediatrician immediately for possible urinary issues.

Q70: When is the ideal time to perform newborn circumcision?

A) Within the first 24 hours after birth

B) Between 2 and 4 weeks of age

C) After the baby reaches 6 months old

Q71: A newborn is having difficulty falling asleep. What comfort measure can the nurse suggest to the parents?

A) Place the baby on their stomach to sleep.

B) Create a soothing bedtime routine, such as dimming the lights and playing soft music.

C) Allow the baby to sleep in a room with bright lights and background noise.

Q72: A newborn is experiencing gas and discomfort. What comfort measure can the nurse recommend to the parents?

A) Use over-the-counter gas relief drops for infants.

B) Lay the baby flat on their back immediately after feeding.

C) Burp the baby after each feeding.

Q73: A nurse is educating parents about safe car seat practices. Which statement by the parents indicates a need for further education?

A) We'll put the car seat in the front seat so we can keep an eye on the baby."

B) "The car seat should be installed in a rear-facing position in the back seat."

C) "We will make sure the car seat is secured tightly with the seatbelt or LATCH system."

Q74: What is the primary purpose of newborn screening for critical congenital heart disease (CCHD)?

A) To identify infants at risk of car seat-related injuries

B) To diagnose cardiac abnormalities in newborns

C) To detect congenital heart defects before they become life-threatening

Q75: A newborn is diagnosed with erythema toxic. How should the nurse educate the parents about this condition?

A) It is a contagious skin infection that requires isolation.

B) It is a rash caused by an allergic reaction to formula milk.

C) It is a common newborn rash that will resolve on its own.

Q76: To prevent skin dryness in a newborn, what is the best recommendation for the parents?

A) Use talcum powder on the baby's skin after bathing.

B) Avoid moisturizers and oils to prevent clogging the pores.

C) Apply a gentle, hypoallergenic moisturizer after bathing.

Q77: What is the recommended age for starting tummy time with a newborn?

A) 1 week old

B) 2 months old

C) 6 months old

Q78: Which of the following safety measures should be taken when using a car seat for a newborn?

A) We'll position the car seat on the front seat of the car.

B) Buckling the car seat with the baby facing forward.

C) Positioning the car seat in the rear-facing position in the back seat.

Q79: What is the purpose of administering eye prophylaxis to a newborn shortly after birth?

A) To prevent infection of the eyes

B) To improve vision in the newborn

C) To reduce the possibility of jaundice

Q80: Which of the following medications is used for passive immunity in newborns born to hepatitis B-positive mothers?

A) HBIG (Hepatitis B Immune Globulin)

B) Oral Sucrose

C) Analgesics

Q81: Which heart rate range indicates the need for chest compressions during newborn resuscitation?

A) 60-80 beats per minute

B) 80-100 beats per minute

C) Above 100 beats per minute

Q82: What is the purpose of administering positive pressure ventilation (PPV) during newborn resuscitation?

A) To improve the newborn's oxygen saturation

B) To prevent heat loss in the newborn

C) To promote early breastfeeding

Q83: If a newborn is not breathing or has inadequate respiratory efforts, what is the next appropriate step in the management of resuscitation?

A) Providing tactile stimulation

B) Administering positive pressure ventilation (PPV)

C) Giving chest compressions

Q84: What is the recommended chest compression-to-ventilation ratio during newborn resuscitation when chest compressions are indicated?

A) 3:1

B) 15:2

C) 30:2

Q85: What medication is typically given to newborns as eye prophylaxis to prevent neonatal conjunctivitis?

A) Tetracycline ointment

B) Erythromycin ointment

C) Ciprofloxacin drops

Q86: What drug is administered to newborns born to mothers with hepatitis B to provide passive immunity against the virus?

A) Hepatitis B vaccine

B) Immunoglobulins (HBIG)

C) Hepatitis C vaccine

Q87: A term newborn with hypothermia receives radiant warmers and skin-to-skin contact with the mother. How can effectiveness of these interventions be evaluated?

A) Increased heart rate

B) Shivering response

C) Stable body temperature

Q88: A newborn with suspected sepsis receives antibiotic therapy. How can the effectiveness of the treatment be assessed?

A) Increased respiratory rate

B) Improved feeding tolerance

C) Persistence of fever

Q89: A newborn receives the following Apgar scores: 8 at 1 minute and 9 at 5 minutes. What do these scores indicate?

A) The newborn requires immediate resuscitation.

B) The newborn is in good overall condition.

C) The newborn needs further evaluation for potential complications.

Q90: A newborn receives the following Apgar scores: 4 at 1 minute and 6 at 5 minutes. What action should the healthcare team take?

A) Prepare for immediate resuscitation.

B) Administer vitamin K injection.

C) Schedule a follow-up visits in a week.

Q91: Which medication is often administered as the first-line treatment for postpartum hemorrhage to promote uterine contractions?

A) Oxytocin

B) Methylergonovine

C) Misoprostol

Q92: Which maternal condition can increase the risk of postpartum hemorrhage?

A) Gestational diabetes

B) Preeclampsia

C) Iron deficiency anemia

Q93: Thrombophlebitis can lead to a serious complication called pulmonary embolism, which is a blockage of blood flow to the:

A) Heart

B) Lungs

C) Brain

Q94: Women with thrombophlebitis are often prescribed anticoagulant medications to:

A) Prevent infection

B) Relieve pain

C) Prevent blood clot enlargement

Q95: Which of the following nursing interventions is important in the care of a woman with thrombophlebitis?

A) Encouraging frequent ambulation

B) Applying heat to the affected leg

C) Elevating the affected leg

Q96: Which of the following symptom's commonly associated with pulmonary embolism?

A) Swollen ankles and feet

B) Difficulty breathing and chest pain

C) Headache and dizziness

Q97: The condition in which a blood clot forms within a deep vein, typically in the legs, is known as:

A) Postpartum hemorrhage

B) Pulmonary embolism

C) Deep vein thrombosis DVT

Q98: Which of the following laboratory findings is commonly seen in a patient with DIC?

A) Elevated platelet count

B) Prolonged clotting times

C) Low blood glucose levels

Q99: The pathophysiology of DIC involves the release of large amounts of:

A) Red blood cells

B) Clotting factors

C) Fetal hemoglobin

Q100: HELLP syndrome is characterized by:

A) Excessive clotting leading to deep vein thrombosis

B) Liver dysfunction and decreased blood clotting ability

C) High-grade fever and sepsis

Q101: What is the recommended management for a woman with severe HELLP syndrome?

A) Immediate induction of labor or cesarean delivery

B) Administration of oral antibiotics

C) Bed rest and increased fluid intake

Q102: A perineal hematoma can result in:

A) Elevated blood pressure

B) Difficulty breathing

C) Severe pain and swelling in the perineal area

Q103: Which intervention is typically required for a large or symptomatic hematoma?

A) Bed rest and hydration

B) Warm compress application

C) Drainage and surgical repair

Q104: A hematoma that forms between the skull and the dura mater is known as:

A) Subarachnoid hematoma

B) Subdural hematoma

C) Intracerebral hematoma

Q105: Which antihypertensive medication is commonly used for managing chronic hypertension during pregnancy?

A) Angiotensin-converting enzyme ACE inhibitors

B) Beta-blockers

C) Diuretics

Q106: Women with chronic hypertension may need more frequent prenatal visits to monitor:

A) Fetal growth and development

B) Maternal weight gain

C) Fluid intake and output

Q107: What is the recommended mode of delivery for women with well-controlled chronic hypertension?

A) Vaginal delivery

B) Elective cesarean section

C) Forceps-assisted delivery

Q108: Gestational hypertension may increase the risk of developing what condition later in life?

A) Type 1 diabetes

B) Cardiovascular disease

C) Osteoporosis

Q109: Women with gestational hypertension are at increased risk of developing what serious complication during pregnancy?

A) Preterm birth

B) Gestational diabetes

C) Anemia

Q110: The mainstay of treatment for eclampsia is:

A) Antibiotics

B) Antihypertensive medications

C) Magnesium sulfate

Q111: Magnesium sulfate is used in eclampsia to:

A) Lower maternal blood pressure

B) Prevent seizures and reduce the risk of cerebral complications

C) Induce labor

Q112: What is the most common route of infection leading to endometritis in the postpartum period?

A. Ascending infection from the lower genital tract

B. Hematogenous spread from distant infection

C. Direct contact with contaminated objects

Q113: Postpartum endometritis is usually diagnosed within how many days after childbirth?

A. 24 hours

B. 72 hours

C. 1 week

Q114: A postpartum woman with a wound infection may exhibit which of the following systemic signs?

A. Elevated blood pressure

B. Increased urinary output

C. Fever and chills

Q115: What is the primary mode of transmission for wound infections in the postpartum period?

A. Airborne transmission

B. Contact with contaminated objects

C. Ingestion of contaminated food

Q116: The nurse observes purulent drainage from a postpartum woman's wound. What is the most appropriate action?

A. Notify the healthcare provider immediately

B. Collect a wound culture for further evaluation

C. Document the finding as a normal postpartum occurrence

Q117: What is the primary causative organism responsible for septic pelvic thrombophlebitis?

A. Escherichia coli (E. coli)

B. Group B Streptococcus (GBS)

C. Staphylococcus aureus

Q118: The nurse suspects septic pelvic thrombophlebitis in a postpartum woman. Which diagnostic test is most appropriate for confirming the diagnosis?

A. Magnetic resonance imaging MRI of the pelvis

B. Complete blood count (CBC) with differential

C. Duplex ultrasound of the affected area

Q119: What is the mainstay of treatment for septic pelvic thrombophlebitis?

A. Intravenous fluids or pain management

B. Antibiotic therapy and anticoagulation

C. Bed rest and warm compresses

Q120: A postpartum woman with a urinary tract infection may experience which of the following symptoms?

A. Constipation and abdominal cramps

B. Nausea and vomiting

C. Lower abdominal pain and cloudy urine

Q121: What is the primary method of diagnosing a urinary tract infection in postpartum woman?

A. Urinalysis and urine culture

B. Blood culture

C. Vaginal swab culture

Q122: A postpartum woman is prescribed antibiotics for a urinary tract infection. What information should the nurse provide regarding medication compliance?

A. "Stop taking the antibiotics once you feel better to avoid side effects."

B. "Take the antibiotics with an empty stomach to enhance absorption."

C. "Complete the full course of antibiotics as prescribed by your healthcare provider."

Q123: The nurse is educating a woman with gestational diabetes about postpartum diabetes management. Which statement by the woman indicates a need for further teaching?

A. "I'll continue to monitor my blood sugar levels regularly after childbirth."

B. "I should stop taking my diabetes medications as soon as I deliver the baby."

C. "A healthy diet and daily exercise can help control my blood sugar levels."

Q124: During the postpartum period, which complication is a potential concern for a woman with pre-existing diabetes?

A. Hypertension

B. Deep vein thrombosis

C. Diabetic ketoacidosis

Q125: A postpartum woman mentions feeling extremely fatigued, sad, and hopeless for the past two weeks. What should the nurse suspect have based on these symptoms?

A. Postpartum depression

B. Postpartum anxiety disorder

C. Postpartum psychosis

Q126: Which action is appropriate for the nurse to take when caring for a postpartum woman with sleep disturbances and signs of postpartum depression?

A. Encourage the woman to engage in social activities to reduce feelings of isolation.

B. I suggest trying over-the-counter sleep medications to enhance sleep quality.

C. Advise the woman to avoid discussing her feelings to prevent further distress.

Q127: The nurse is assessing a postpartum woman for substance use disorders. Which statement is true regarding substance use during pregnancy and its impact on sleep disturbances in the postpartum period?

A. Substance use during pregnancy does not impact sleep patterns in the postpartum period.

B. Using substances during pregnancy may cause sleep disturbances after childbirth.

C. Sleep disturbances in the postpartum period are solely related to hormonal changes.

Q128: What is a significant concern for a woman experiencing postpartum psychosis?

A. Increased risk of substance use disorder

B. Potential harm to herself or her infant

C. Development of bipolar disorder

Q129: The nurse is providing education to a postpartum woman with postpartum depression. Which statement indicates a need for further teaching?

A. "I should talk to my healthcare provider about counseling and support options."

B. "I can continue taking my prescribed antidepressant medication while breastfeeding."

C. "I'll stop attending social events to avoid feeling overwhelmed."

Q130: A postpartum woman with postpartum depression expresses feelings of guilt and worthlessness. What is the most appropriate nursing response?

A. "It's normal to feel this way after childbirth. These feelings will pass on their own."

B. "You shouldn't be feeling this way. Try to focus on the positive aspects of motherhood."

C. "It must be challenging for you. I'm here to listen and support you through this."

Q131: The nurse is caring for a newborn whose mother has a history of substance abuse. Which nursing intervention is essential for monitoring the newborn's well-being?

A. Frequent breastfeeding to promote bonding

B. Performing a toxicology screening on the newborn

C. Encouraging rooming-in with the mother

Q132: A postpartum woman is admitted to the maternity unit with suspected substance abuse. What should be the priority of care for the nurse?

A. Encouraging the woman to seek counseling after discharge

B. Providing education on the risks of substance abuse during pregnancy

C. Ensuring the safety of the woman and her newborn

Q133: What is the primary pathophysiological characteristic of cyanotic heart disease?

A. Increased pulmonary blood flow

B. Obstruction of blood flow from the heart

C. Mixing of oxygenated and deoxygenated blood in the heart

Q134: A newborn is diagnosed with transposition of the great arteries (TGA). Which intervention is the priority in the immediate management of this condition?

A. Administering prostaglandin E1 (PGE1) infusion

B. Preparing for corrective surgery within the next 48 hours

C. Initiating enteral feedings to improve oxygenation

Q135: A newborn is suspected to have hypoplastic left heart syndrome (HLHS). Which assessment finding would be consistent with this condition?

A. Strong peripheral pulses and bounding pulse pressure

B. Harsh systolic murmur and bounding pulses

C. Weak or absent femoral pulses and cool lower extremities

Q136: A newborn presents with a loud, harsh murmur and bounding pulses. Which a cyanotic heart defect is the most likely cause of these findings?

A. Coarctation of the aorta (CoA)

B. Atrial septal defect (ASD)

C. Pulmonary stenosis

Q137: A neonate is diagnosed with apnea of prematurity. What intervention is most appropriate to manage this condition?

A. Administering intravenous antibiotics

B. Placing the neonate in an incubator

C. Providing continuous positive airway pressure (CPAP)

Q138: A full-term newborn presents with rapid, shallow breathing, and mild retractions shortly after birth. The chest X-ray shows increased lung fluid. What is the most appropriate intervention for this newborn?

A. Initiate antibiotics to treat a possible infection

B. Administer surfactant replacement therapy

C. Administer oxygen therapy to maintain oxygen saturation

Q139: A term newborn is showing signs of respiratory distress, such as rapid breathing, grunting, and retractions. On auscultation, decreased breath sounds are noted on one side of the chest. What could be a potential cause of these findings?

A. Transient Tachypnea of the Newborn (TTN)

B. Meconium aspiration syndrome

C. Pneumothorax

Q140: A newborn is born with signs of meconium aspiration syndrome. What characteristic finding is typically seen on a chest X-ray in a neonate with meconium aspiration?

A. Hyperinflated lungs

B. Ground-glass appearance

C. Fluid-filled lungs

Q141: A full-term newborn is brought to the neonatal unit with suspected seizures. The nurse is assessing the baby and notices the presence of irregular, repetitive, and stereotyped movements. The baby is not responding to stimuli during these episodes. What type of seizures does this presentation suggest?

A. Absence seizures

B. Tonic seizures

C. Myoclonic seizures

Q142: A full-term newborn presents with jitteriness and poor feeding. The mother has a history of diabetes. Which of the following conditions should the nurse suspect in this newborn?

A. Neonatal sepsis

B. Hypoglycemia

C. Neonatal abstinence syndrome

Q143: A premature newborn is at possibility for intracranial hemorrhage due to the fragility of blood vessels in the brain. Which of the following factors contributes to this vulnerability?

A. Adequate oxygen saturation

B. Well-developed blood-brain barrier

C. Immature blood vessel structure

Q144: The nurse is conducting a prenatal education class for expectant mothers. What advice should the nurse provide to prevent neural tube defects in newborns?

A. Encourage regular consumption of foods rich in folic acid during pregnancy.

B. Advise expectant mothers to avoid sunlight exposure to prevent NTDs.

C. Recommend complete bed rest during the first trimester of pregnancy to reduce the possibility of NTDs.

Q145: A pregnant woman with a history of substance abuse seeks prenatal care. What is the nurse's priority intervention to improve outcomes for the newborn?

A. Administering opioid antagonists immediately after birth.

B. Encouraging the woman to stop all substance use immediately.

C. Collaborating with a social worker to create a support plan for the mother and newborn.

Q146: A newborn is diagnosed with imperforate anus. Which nursing intervention is a priority for this newborn?

A. Initiating bowel training exercises immediately after birth.

B. Placing a nasogastric tube to decompress the bowel.

C. Administering antibiotics to prevent infection.

Q147: A newborn is diagnosed with esophageal atresia and tracheoesophageal fistula (TEF). The nurse understands that the primary concern related to this condition is:

A. The risk of aspiration and pneumonia.

B. Failure to thrive due to malabsorption.

C. Neurological complications.

Q148: A preterm newborn is at risk for anemia due to decreased erythropoietin production. Which intervention would be beneficial in reducing the risk of anemia in this neonate?

A. Early umbilical cord clamping

B. Delayed umbilical cord clamping

C. Routine administration of iron supplements

Q149: A nurse is caring for a newborn who exhibits easy bruising and bleeding from the umbilical cord stump. The mother reports that she had a strict vegetarian diet during pregnancy. The nurse suspects a deficiency of which vitamin in the newborn?

A. Vitamin A

B. Vitamin C

C. Vitamin K

Q150: A newborn is diagnosed with vitamin K deficiency bleeding. The nurse explains to the parents that this condition occurs due to insufficient levels of clotting factors. Which clotting factor is primarily affected in vitamin K deficiency?

A. Factor VIII

B. Factor IX

C. Factor VII

Q151: A newborn's hyperbilirubinemia is severe and requires treatment to prevent complications. What's the common treatment method for neonatal hyperbilirubinemia?

A. Intravenous antibiotics

B. Phototherapy

C. Oxygen supplementation

Q152: A newborn is diagnosed with ABO incompatibility, and the healthcare provider orders a bilirubin level test to monitor the baby's condition. What type of jaundice is commonly associated with ABO incompatibility?

A. Physiologic jaundice

B. Pathologic jaundice

C. Indirect jaundice

Q153: A nurse is caring for a newborn with ABO incompatibility. Which intervention is a priority in the management of this condition?

A. Administering vitamin K to prevent bleeding

B. Providing phototherapy to reduce bilirubin levels

C. Initiating intravenous (IV) fluid therapy

Q154: A newborn is diagnosed with hemolytic disease due to Rh incompatibility. Which intervention is essential to prevent further complications in the baby?

A. Providing phototherapy to reduce bilirubin levels

B. Administering intravenous (IV) fluids for hydration

C. Initiating breastfeeding immediately after birth

Q155: G6PD deficiency can lead to hemolysis of red blood cells, causing anemia. Which of the following physical findings might be observed in a neonate with G6PD deficiency during a hemolytic crisis?

A. Jaundice and pale skin

B. Cyanosis and labored breathing

C. Petechiae and purpura on the skin

Q156: A mother is concerned about her newborn's G6PD deficiency and asks if it will be a lifelong condition. How should the nurse respond?

A. "G6PD deficiency is only a temporary condition that resolves on its own."

B. "The condition is lifelong, but with proper management, your baby can lead a normal life."

C. "G6PD deficiency is a severe condition that may shorten your baby's lifespan."

Q157: A newborn is diagnosed with polycythemia. Which of the following complications is a potential concern in this condition due to increased blood viscosity?

A. Increased risk of infection

B. Risk of hypoglycemia

C. Increased risk of thrombosis

Q158: The nurse is caring for a neonate with polycythemia. Which of the following interventions is appropriate to manage polycythemia in the newborn?

A. Administering intravenous iron supplements

B. Providing frequent small feedings of glucose water

C. Initiating phototherapy for hyperbilirubinemia

Q159: A neonate is diagnosed with hyper viscosity, and the healthcare provider orders a partial exchange transfusion. What is the primary goal of a partial exchange transfusion in a neonate with hyper viscosity?

A. To increase the level of white blood cells

B. To decrease the bilirubin levels in the blood

C. To reduce the total volume of blood in circulation

Q160: Thrombocytopenia's defined as a low platelet count in the blood. What is the normal platelet count range for a term neonate?

A. 100,000 to 200,000/mm³

B. 150,000 to 300,000/mm³

C. 200,000 to 400,000/mm³

Q161: Which of the following is a common early clinical manifestation of neonatal sepsis?

A. Bradycardia

B. Hypoglycemia

C. Hyperbilirubinemia

Q162: A newborn presents with petechiae, purpura, and prolonged bleeding from minor injuries. Which laboratory finding is most likely to be abnormal in this baby with suspected hemostatic disorders?

A. Elevated Hemoglobin (Hb) level

B. Decreased Platelet count

C. Increased White Blood Cell (WBC) count

Q163: In a newborn with suspected viral infection, which parameter from the CBC and differential is crucial to monitor for potential complications related to viral replication and immune response?

A. Hemoglobin (Hb) level

B. White Blood Cell (WBC) count

C. Platelet count

Q164: A newborn is scheduled for a lumbar puncture. What position should the maternal nurse instruct the parents to place the baby during the procedure?

A. Prone (face down)

B. Supine (face up)

C. Lateral recumbent (on the side)

Q165: During a lumbar puncture on a neonate, the maternal nurse observes clear cerebrospinal fluid (CSF) coming from the needle. What should be the appropriate nursing action?

A. Document the finding and notify the healthcare provider

B. Administer antibiotics immediately

C. Stop the procedure and reposition the baby

Q166: A neonate presents with a characteristic "slapped cheek" rash on the face and body. The maternal nurse suspects a viral infection. Which virus is the likely cause of this condition?

A. Measles virus

B. Rubella virus

C. Parvovirus B19

Q167: A newborn is experiencing signs of sepsis, including fever, irritability, and poor feeding. The maternal nurse suspects an STI transmitted vertically from the mother during pregnancy. Which STI is most likely responsible for these symptoms?

A. Trichomoniasis

B. Hepatitis B virus (HBV)

C. Human immunodeficiency virus (HIV)

Q168: A neonate presents with a characteristic "strawberry tongue" and a fever. The maternal nurse suspects an STI transmitted from the mother during birth. Which STI is the likely cause of these findings?

A. Herpes simplex virus (HSV)

B. Human papillomavirus (HPV)

C. Group B Streptococcus (GBS)

Q169: A neonate with a confirmed bacterial infection is receiving an aminoglycoside antibiotic. The maternal nurse closely monitors the neonate's renal function. What is the rationale for this monitoring?

A. Aminoglycosides can cause hepatotoxicity.

B. Aminoglycosides can cause bone marrow suppression.

C. Aminoglycosides can cause nephrotoxicity.

Answer: C. Aminoglycosides can cause nephrotoxicity.

Q170: A pregnant woman is diagnosed with a group B streptococcal infection, and intrapartum antibiotics are administered. Why is intrapartum antibiotic prophylaxis crucial in this situation?

A. To prevent the transmission of infection from the mother to the neonate during childbirth.

B. To treat the neonate's infection after birth.

C. To prevent postpartum hemorrhage in the mother.

Q171: A neonate is born with a genetic disorder that affects insulin production, leading to persistent hypoglycemia. The healthcare provider prescribes a continuous intravenous infusion of glucose to manage the condition. As the maternal nurse, your priority is to monitor the neonate closely for which potential complication related to this treatment?

A. Hyperglycemia

B. Hypertension

C. Infection at the infusion site

Q172: A newborn is diagnosed with a rare genetic disorder affecting carbohydrate metabolism. The infant presents with failure to thrive, lethargy, and a distinctive "musty" odor to the skin. Which of the following is the most likely inborn error of metabolism responsible for these clinical manifestations?

A. Phenylketonuria (PKU)

B. Galactosemia

C. Maple syrup urine disease (MSUD)

Q173: A newborn is diagnosed with a rare genetic disorder caused by a mutation on the X chromosome. The father does not have the disease, but the mother is a carrier. What is the likelihood that this couple's future sons will inherit the disease?

A. 0%

B. 25%

C. 50%

Q174: A nurse is caring for an infant of a diabetic mother in the neonatal intensive care unit NICU. The baby is showing signs of respiratory distress shortly after birth. Which of the following conditions should the nurse suspect in this infant?

A. Respiratory distress syndrome RDS

B. Transient tachypnea of the newborn (TTN)

C. Meconium aspiration syndrome (MAS)

Q175: A term newborn is diagnosed with hypoglycemia. The healthcare provider orders glucose gel to be administered to the baby. How should the nurse administer the glucose gel to the newborn?

A. By placing a few drops on the baby's tongue

B. By adding it to the baby's feeding bottle

C. By rubbing it on the baby's skin

D. By mixing it with breast milk and feeding it through a syringe

Test 6 Answer Key

1	C	27	C	53	C
2	C	28	C	54	B
3	C	29	A	55	B
4	C	30	A	56	B
5	A	31	B	57	B
6	B	32	B	58	B
7	A	33	B	59	B
8	C	34	B	60	B
9	B	35	C	61	C
10	A	36	C	62	C
11	A	37	C	63	B
12	A	38	C	64	B
13	B	39	B	65	A
14	A	40	C	66	A
15	B	41	B	67	A
16	B	42	B	68	B
17	C	43	B	69	A
18	C	44	A	70	B
19	A	45	C	71	B
20	A	46	A	72	C
21	A	47	C	73	A
22	B	48	C	74	C
23	C	49	B	75	C
24	B	50	C	76	C
25	B	51	B	77	A
26	B	52	C	78	C

79	A		106	A		133	C
80	A		107	A		134	A
81	A		108	B		135	C
82	A		109	A		136	A
83	B		110	C		137	C
84	C		111	B		138	C
85	B		112	A		139	C
86	B		113	B		140	B
87	C		114	C		141	A
88	B		115	B		142	B
89	B		116	B		143	C
90	A		117	C		144	A
91	A		118	C		145	C
92	B		119	B		146	B
93	B		120	C		147	A
94	C		121	A		148	B
95	A		122	C		149	C
96	B		123	B		150	C
97	C		124	C		151	B
98	B		125	A		152	B
99	B		126	A		153	B
100	B		127	B		154	A
101	A		128	B		155	A
102	C		129	C		156	B
103	C		130	C		157	C
104	B		131	B		158	B
105	B		132	C		159	C

160	B	166	C	172	C
161	A	167	C	173	B
162	B	168	C	174	A
163	B	169	C	175	A
164	C	170	A		
165	A	171	A		

Maternal Newborn Nursing Exam Practice Test 7

Q 1: During an antenatal class, a pregnant woman asks about the purpose of Kegel exercises during pregnancy. What is the nurse's best response?

A. "Kegel exercises help strengthen the abdominal muscles."

B. "Kegel exercises can reduce the risk of gestational diabetes."

C. "Kegel exercises help strengthen the pelvic floor muscles, which can support the bladder and uterus."

Q 2: During a childbirth education class, a pregnant woman in her mid-40s asks about potential complications during pregnancy due to her age. The nurse should educate her about the increased risk of which antenatal complication associated with advanced maternal age?

A. Preterm labor and delivery

B. Gestational diabetes mellitus (GDM)

C. Placenta previa

Q3: During a routine prenatal checkup a pregnant woman in her second trimester asks about the importance of omega-3 fatty acids during pregnancy. What key benefits can omega 3 fatty acids provide to the developing fetus and the mother during pregnancy?

A. Enhancing fetal bone development

B. Reducing the risk of preterm labor

C. Promoting healthy brain and eye development

Q4: A pregnant woman reports a history of three previous deliveries via cesarean section. What antenatal consideration should the nurse keep in mind, given this obstetrical history factor?

A. High risk of gestational diabetes mellitus GDM

B. Increased likelihood of preterm labor

C. Potential for uterine rupture during labor

Q5: During an antenatal visit, a pregnant woman discusses the importance of family involvement during labor and childbirth in her cultural tradition. What psychosocial/cultural issue should the nurse recognize to support the woman's cultural preferences and promote family-centered care?

A. Accepting the woman's desire for home birth

B. Encouraging early epidural analgesia for pain relief

C. Allowing the presence of family members in the labor room

Q6: A pregnant woman presents for an antenatal check-up and discloses a history of pelvic inflammatory disease (PID) with previous sexually transmitted infections. What antenatal factor should the healthcare provider consider as a potential risk in this pregnancy?

A. Gestational diabetes mellitus GDM

B. Premature rupture of membranes (PROM)

C. Ectopic pregnancy

Q7: A pregnant woman's undergoing routine laboratory testing during her antenatal check-up. Her blood test reveals a decreased hemoglobin level within the normal range for pregnancy. What antenatal consideration should the nurse discuss with the woman based on this finding?

A. Risk of iron deficiency anemia

B. Need for immediate blood transfusion

C. Increased possibility of preeclampsia

Q8: A pregnant woman with a history of multiple miscarriages is worried about the possibility of another miscarriage in her current pregnancy. What antepartum intervention can provide reassurance and support to the woman during this time?

A. Increased physical activity

B. Frequent ultrasound examinations

C. High-dose vitamin supplementation

Q9: A pregnant woman at 34 weeks of gestation presents with sudden-onset severe abdominal pain and vaginal bleeding. She also reports that her baby's movements have decreased significantly. What antepartum complication should the healthcare provider consider as an urgent concern for this woman?

A. Placental abruption

B. Preterm labor

C. Gestational diabetes mellitus (GDM)

Q10 A pregnant woman at 32 weeks of gestation is concerned about her baby's growth and development. The healthcare provider recommends an ultrasound to assess fetal growth. What parameter is commonly measured during this assessment?

A. Fetal heart rate

B. Fetal lung maturity

C. Fetal biometry

Q11: A pregnant woman who had bariatric surgery in the past is concerned about the risk of nutritional deficiencies during her pregnancy. What nutrient should the healthcare provider monitor closely in this woman's prenatal care?

A. Vitamin C

B. Folic acid

C. Vitamin D

Q12: A laboring woman's fetal heart rate pattern shows prolonged decelerations on the monitor strip. What does this pattern indicate, and how should the nurse respond?

A. Prolonged decelerations indicate a vagal response, and the nurse should encourage the mother to breathe deeply and slowly.

B. Prolonged decelerations are a normal finding during active labor, and no intervention is required.

C. Prolonged decelerations indicate a potential problem with fetal oxygenation, and the nurse should reposition the mother, administer oxygen, and notify the healthcare provider.

Q13: Postpartum hemorrhage is a potential complication following childbirth. What vital sign indicates early postpartum hemorrhage and requires close monitoring?

A. Decreased urinary output

B. Elevated blood pressure

C. Increased uterine tone

Q14: A postpartum woman is experiencing excessive swelling of her lower extremities. Which intervention should the nurse prioritize to alleviate the edema?

A. Encouraging increased fluid intake

B. Elevating the legs above the heart level

C. Applying warm compresses to the swollen areas

Q15: During the postpartum period, the maternal cardiovascular system undergoes significant changes. What usual physical changes happen in women after childbirth?

A. Decreased cardiac output

B. Increased blood pressure

C. Decreased blood volume

Q16: A postpartum woman complains of perineal pain and discomfort. Upon physical assessment, the nurse notes swelling and bruising in the perineal area. Which of the following interventions should the nurse recommend to alleviate the woman's discomfort?

A. Application of cold packs to the perineum

B. Encouraging the woman to sit for prolonged periods

C. Avoiding the use of pain medication

Q17: A postpartum woman complains of abdominal distention and gas pain after delivery. Which of the following nursing interventions would be most appropriate to alleviate the woman's discomfort?

A. Encouraging the woman to limit fluid intake

B. Administering over-the-counter antacids

C. Encouraging ambulation and gentle movement

Q18: A postpartum woman presents with symptoms of gastroesophageal reflux disease GERD including heartburn and regurgitation. Which of the following nursing interventions should be included in the woman's care plan?

A. Encouraging the woman to lie down immediately after meals

B. Recommending a diet high in spicy and acidic foods

C. Elevating the head of the bed during sleep

Q19: Which of the following laboratory tests is commonly used to assess a postpartum woman's coagulation status and the risk of bleeding?

A. Complete blood count (CBC)

B. Prothrombin time (PT)

C. Blood glucose level

Q20: Which of the following hormones is responsible for promoting lactation and milk production in a breastfeeding woman?

A. Prolactin

B. Progesterone

C. Human chorionic gonadotropin (chg.)

Q21: A postpartum woman is at possibility for thrombophlebitis due to decreased mobility during the immediate postpartum period. Which nursing intervention is essential in preventing thrombophlebitis?

A. Administering prophylactic antibiotics to prevent infection.

B. Encouraging frequent ambulation and leg exercises.

C. Applying cold packs to the lower extremities to reduce inflammation.

Q22: A postpartum woman has been experiencing excessive perineal pain and discomfort. Upon assessment, the nurse observes that the perineal pad is saturated with bright red lochia and there is a sudden gush of blood when the woman stands up. What action should the nurse take in response to these findings?

A. Document the findings as a normal postpartum occurrence.

B Tell the woman to do Kegel exercises for strengthening her pelvic floor muscles.

C. Notify the healthcare provider immediately as it may indicate postpartum hemorrhage.

Q23: A baby's born to a mother who has been diagnosed with HIV. What medication should the neonate receive shortly after birth to reduce the risk of HIV transmission?

A. Vaccines

B. Antiretroviral

C. Methadone (Subutex) SSI's

Q24: A postpartum woman is experiencing persistent constipation. Which class of medication can be prescribed to improve gastrointestinal motility?

A. Diuretics

B. Antimicrobials

C. GI Motility Drugs

Q25: A newborn is born to a mother who is Rh-negative. The nurse prepares to administer Rh immune globulin (RhoGAM) to the mother. When should the nurse administer RhoGAM to the Rh-negative mother to prevent Rh isoimmunization in subsequent pregnancies?

A. Before delivery

B. Within 24 hours postpartum

C. Two weeks after delivery

Q26: A pregnant woman with a history of epilepsy's prescribed an antiepileptic drug to manage her seizures. Which counseling point should the nurse prioritize when discussing this medication with the woman?

A. Potential increased risk of gestational diabetes

B. Possible interference with fetal bone development

C. Increased likelihood of multiple gestation

Q27: A breastfeeding mother is prescribed a medication from the antiretroviral class. What is a critical aspect of patient education that the nurse should emphasize for the lactating woman?

A. "Antiretroviral medications may reduce your milk production, so supplement with formula as needed."

B. "Continue breastfeeding, as antiretroviral medications do not transfer into breast milk and are safe for your baby."

C. "Interrupt breastfeeding while taking antiretroviral medications to avoid transmitting the virus to your baby."

Q28: A pregnant woman with gestational diabetes is prescribed insulin therapy. What critical teaching point should the nurse emphasize regarding insulin administration during pregnancy?

A. "You should only administer insulin if your blood glucose levels are very high."

B. "Insulin needs may decrease as pregnancy progresses, so monitor your blood glucose levels regularly."

C. "Avoid injecting insulin into the abdominal region during pregnancy to prevent harm to the fetus."

Q29: A postpartum woman reports experiencing urinary retention and difficulty emptying her bladder. What nursing intervention is appropriate to address this common problem?

A. Encourage the woman to drink plenty of fluids to promote bladder emptying.

B. Catheterize the woman to relieve bladder distention.

C. Assist the woman to the bathroom and provide privacy for voiding.

Q30: A postpartum woman complains of severe headache that worsens when sitting or standing upright. What common problem should the nurse suspect, and what intervention is appropriate?

A. Suspect spinal headache and encourage the woman to lie flat.

B. Suspect postpartum eclampsia and administer antihypertensive medication.

C. Suspect breast engorgement and apply cold compresses to the forehead.

Q31: A breastfeeding woman is experiencing persistent pain and irritation in her breasts, and her breasts feel swollen and firm. What complication is likely present, and what intervention should the nurse recommend?

A. Afterpains; encourage the woman to use relaxation techniques to manage pain.

B. Perineal edema and pain; advise the woman to sit on a cushioned surface to relieve discomfort.

C. Breast engorgement; encourage frequent breastfeeding and offer warm compresses.

Q32: A postpartum woman asks the nurse about ways to manage perineal pain and discomfort after childbirth. What should the nurse recommend?

A. "You should avoid sitting for extended periods to relieve perineal pain."

B. "Applying a warm compress to the perineal area can help reduce pain and promote healing."

C. "Take over-the-counter pain medication for immediate relief from perineal discomfort."

Q33: A postpartum woman is concerned about her risk of developing hemorrhoids. What patient education should the nurse provide to prevent hemorrhoids?

A. "Eat a diet rich in fiber or drink plenty of fluids to prevent constipation and reduce the risk of hemorrhoids."

B. "Avoid sitting for extended periods to reduce pressure on the rectal area and prevent hemorrhoids."

C. You cannot prevent hemorrhoids, but they typically go away on their own without treatment.

Q34: A breastfeeding woman experiences sore nipples. What advice should the nurse provide to address this issue?

A. Ensure that the infant has a proper latch on to the breast.

B. Limit the feeding time on each breast.

C. Wash her breasts frequently with soap.

Q35: What is the recommended daily intake of elemental iron for a pregnant woman with normal hemoglobin levels?

A. 30 mg of elemental iron

B. 60 mg of elemental iron

C. 120 mg of elemental iron

Q36: Which of the following best describes "Feeding Cues" in the context of breastfeeding?

A. The baby's attachment to the breast during feeding.

B. The signals or signs the baby exhibits when they are hungry and ready to breastfeed.

C. The rhythmic pattern of the baby's mouth movements during feeding.

Q37: When does colostrum, the first milk produced by the breasts after childbirth, typically transition to mature breast milk?

A. 24 hours after birth

B. 48-72 hours after birth

C. One week after birth

Q38: When might hand expression be recommended for a breastfeeding mother?

A. To replace breastfeeding sessions with bottle feeding.

B. To relieve breast engorgement and improve milk flow.

C. As a substitute for using a breast pump.

Q39: A breastfeeding mother is experiencing nipple pain due to cracked nipples. What breast care intervention can be recommended to promote healing and prevent infection?

A. Use of supplementary feedings

B. Use of breastfeeding devices

C. Expressing and storing breast milk

Q40: A breastfeeding mother is struggling with low milk supply. Which breast care intervention can help increase milk production and maintain breastfeeding?

A. Use of supplementary feedings

B. Use of breastfeeding devices

C. Expressing and storing breast milk

Q41: A breastfeeding mother is returning to work and needs to continue breastfeeding her baby. What key point of nipple care should be emphasized in teaching her about expressing and storing breast milk?

A. Ensure frequent and prolonged pumping sessions.

B. Use a manual breast pump for optimal milk expression.

C. Store expressed milk in a clean, sterile container.

Q42: A breastfeeding mother is experiencing cracked and bleeding nipples. What condition would prevent breastfeeding in this situation?

A. Latch on problems

B. Nipple problems

C. Insufficient milk supply

Q43: A breastfeeding mother is a chronic substance abuser and is currently using illicit drugs. . What condition would prevent breastfeeding in this situation?

A. Maternal illness

B. Perinatal substance abuse

C. Insufficient milk supply

Q44: A mother who delivered prematurely is informed that her newborn needs to stay in the neonatal intensive care unit NICU for specialized care. What is the term used to describe the care that involves constant monitoring and treatment for critically ill or premature newborns?

A. Postnatal monitoring

B. Neonatal isolation

C. Neonatal intensive care

Q45: A breastfeeding mother is experiencing sore nipples. Which of the following pieces of advice should the nurse provide to the mother to help alleviate the discomfort?

A. Ensure that the infant has a proper latch on to the breast.

B. Limit the feeding time on each breast.

C. Wash her breasts frequently with soap.

Q46: During pregnancy, a woman's basal metabolic rate (BMR) typically experiences which of the following changes?

A. Decrease

B. Increase

C. Remain stable

Q47: A new mother is feeling overwhelmed and experiencing mood swings after childbirth. What is the most appropriate nursing intervention?

A Suggest medication for treating postpartum depression.

B. Provide emotional support and encouragement.

C. Advise the mother to take on additional responsibilities to improve her mood.

Q48: Which of the following is an appropriate intervention to facilitate bonding and attachment in a family with a preterm newborn in the neonatal intensive care unit NICU?

A. Encouraging parents to minimize their presence in the NICU to reduce stress.

B. Providing opportunities for parents to hold and participate in care for their preterm baby.

C. Discouraging parents from expressing their emotions during the baby's hospital stay.

Q49: Which statement best describes the concept of maternal role attainment?

A. It refers to the process of becoming a mother biologically.

B. It is the achievement of perfection in the maternal role.

C. It encompasses the changes and growth a woman undergoes as she embraces the maternal role.

Q50: What is an essential action for parents to take when addressing sibling rivalry and conflicts between older siblings and the newborn?

A. Reprimand the older siblings for any negative behavior towards the baby.

B. Encourage competition between siblings to build their resilience.

C. Provide opportunities for older siblings to bond with and express love for the newborn.

Q51: How can healthcare providers promote successful parent/infant interactions for a preeclamptic woman in the postpartum period?

A. Encouraging the mother to rest and minimize any physical contact with the newborn.

B. Providing education on the importance of breastfeeding devices to enhance bonding.

C. Facilitating frequent skin-to-skin contact and involving the mother in newborn care.

Q52: Which factor is likely to have the LEAST impact on family integration in the postpartum period?

A. The mother's age at the time of childbirth

B. The type of delivery vaginal or cesarean

C. The baby's gender

Q53: How can healthcare providers address cultural barriers to family integration?

A. By discouraging family members from participating in newborn care

B. By recommending the avoidance of cultural rituals during the postpartum period

C. By providing education and support that aligns with cultural beliefs

Q54: What should healthcare providers do if they suspect a postpartum woman is a victim of intimate partner violence?

A. Report their suspicions to the police without informing the woman.

B. Document the suspicion in the woman's medical record but take no further action.

C. Initiate a non-judgmental conversation with the woman and offer support.

Q55: A postpartum mother expresses concerns about her ability to balance her career and new role as a mother. She worries about how she will manage both responsibilities effectively. What is the most appropriate nursing intervention?

A) Suggesting that she quits her job to focus solely on motherhood.

B) Providing resources and information about work-life balance strategies.

C) Minimizing her concerns and encouraging her to ignore her career worries.

Q56: A mother who is placing her baby for adoption is experiencing grief and emotional distress. How can the nurse assist the mother during this time?

A) Encourage her to suppress her emotions to avoid further distress.

B) Offer counseling and emotional support to help her process her feelings.

C) Advise her to avoid thinking about the adoption to reduce her distress.

Q57: A couple is experiencing perinatal grief after the loss of their baby. How can the nurse promote healthy coping strategies for the couple?

A) Recommend medication to help them manage their grief.

B) Encourage them to isolate themselves from friends and family for some time.

C) Provide resources on support groups and counseling to help them navigate their grief.

Q58: In a resource-limited setting, a postpartum woman is unable to afford necessary postnatal medications and care. How can the ethical principle of justice guide the nurse's actions?

A) Prioritize care for women who can afford the necessary medications and treatments.

B) Advocate for policies that ensure equitable access to essential postnatal care for all women.

C) Inform the woman that she must find a way to pay for the required medications.

Newborn Assessment and Management

Q59: A newborn's blood pressure is measured to be 70/40 mmHg. What action should the nurse take based on this finding?

A) Initiate cardiopulmonary resuscitation CPR immediately.

B) Document the finding as a normal blood pressure for a term newborn.

C) Notify the healthcare provider and monitor the newborn closely.

Q60: A newborn is delivered via vacuum-assisted delivery due to prolonged labor. What is a potential concern related to thermoregulation in this newborn?

A) Increased risk of hypothermia due to the use of vacuum extraction.

B) Decreased risk of heat loss since the birth process was facilitated.

C) Reduced need for immediate skin-to-skin contact with the mother.

Q61: A newborn is suspected to have an infection. Which laboratory test is used to assess for infection in the newborn's bloodstream?

A) Blood culture

B) Urinalysis

C) C-reactive protein CRP level

Q62: A newborn is born preterm and requires supplemental oxygen due to respiratory distress. Which laboratory test is essential to monitor the newborn's oxygen levels and acid-base balance?

A) Liver function tests (LFTs)

B) Arterial blood gas (ABG) analysis

C) Complete blood count (CBC)

Q63: When assessing gestational age using the Ballard Score, which sign assesses the newborn's muscle tone?

A) Scarf sign

B) Popliteal angle

C) Arm recoil

Q64: Which method of gestational age assessment involves measuring specific physical characteristics of the newborn and plotting them on growth charts?

A) Dubowitz Score

B) Ballard Score

C) Caparo Method

Q65: During the sensory assessment of a newborn, which action indicates a normal sense of touch and response to tactile stimuli?

A) Blinking in response to bright light

B) Crying when exposed to a loud noise

C) Clasping their fingers around an examiner's finger

Q66: When assessing the sensory responses of a newborn, which reflex is tested by stroking the sole of the baby's foot from the heel toward the toes?

A) Moro reflex

B) Babinski reflex

C) Rooting reflex

Q67: During a newborn's physical examination, the nurse observes a tuft of hair at the base of the spine. What should the nurse do next?

A) Document the finding and inform the pediatrician.

B) Assess for signs of respiratory distress.

C) Perform a thorough musculoskeletal assessment.

Q68: When assessing a newborn's umbilical cord stump, the nurse notes redness, swelling, and discharge at the base. What action should the nurse take that would be most suitable in this circumstance?

A) Document the findings and continue routine cord care.

B) Apply an antiseptic solution to the cord stump to prevent infection.

C) Notify the healthcare provider immediately for further evaluation and possible treatment.

Q69: A 3-day-old newborn is experiencing constipation, and the mother is concerned. What is the appropriate nursing intervention for the baby's constipation?

A) Administer a glycerin suppository to relieve constipation.

B) Offer water to the baby in addition to breast milk or formula.

C) Encourage the mother to continue breastfeeding and reassure her that newborns may have infrequent bowel movements.

Q70: What is a potential complication that the nurse should monitor for after newborn circumcision?

A) Decreased appetite for breastfeeding

B) Mild redness and swelling at the circumcision site

C) Excessive bleeding or signs of infection

Q71: A newborn is undergoing a painful procedure. What comfort measure can the nurse use to provide comfort during the procedure?

A) Use a distraction technique, such as singing or talking to the baby.

B) Apply a cold compress directly on the procedure site.

C) Encourage the parents to leave the room during the procedure.

Q72: A newborn is exhibiting signs of hunger. What comfort measure can the nurse recommend to the mother?

A) Offer a bottle with diluted infant formula.

B) Delay feeding to establish a strict feeding schedule.

C) Allow the baby to breastfeed on demand.

Q73: When should parents transition their baby from a rear-facing car seat to a forward-facing car seat?

A) At 1 year of age

B) When the baby weighs 20 pounds

C) When the baby reaches the height and weight limits of the rear-facing car seat

Q74: During a newborn's car seat inspection, the nurse notices that the car seat is installed too loosely. What should the nurse advise the parents to do?

A) Tighten the straps until they are snug against the baby's body.

B) Place a soft cushion under the baby's head for added support.

C) Use a rolled-up towel to adjust the angle of the car seat for a better fit.

Q75: A newborn is born with Mongolian spots on the back and buttocks. What should the nurse do?

A) Document the findings, as these are benign birthmarks.

B) Initiate further evaluation and notify the pediatrician.

C) Apply a topical cream to lighten the birthmarks.

Q76: How should parents be instructed to clean the umbilical cord stump of their newborn?

A) Clean the base of the stump with alcohol after each diaper change.

B) Avoid touching the cord stump until it falls off naturally.

C) Clean the stump with soap and water during each bath.

Q77: What should parents be advised to avoid in the baby's sleep area to reduce the risk of suffocation?

A) Soft bedding, such as pillows and quilts.

B) Stuffed animals and toys.

C) Dim lighting in the room.

Q78: When should a baby be transitioned from a bassinet to a crib?

A) As soon as they weigh 5 pounds.

B) When they can roll from side to back.

C) When they reach 6 months of age.

Q79: When are vaccines usually administered to newborns to protect against infectious diseases?

A) Before discharge from the hospital

B) During the first week after birth

C) At six months of age

Q80: What is the primary purpose of administering analgesics to newborns?

A) To induce sleep

B) To provide pain relief

C) To increase appetite

Answer: B) To provide pain relief

Q81: Which of the following is a risk factor that may predispose a newborn to require resuscitation?

A) Full-term gestation

B) Spontaneous vaginal delivery

C) Meconium-stained amniotic fluid

Q82: How long should initial resuscitative efforts be provided before considering discontinuing resuscitation for a newborn who does not respond?

A) 1 minute

B) 5 minutes

C) 10 minutes

Q83: In the "ABC" approach, what does "C" stand for?

A) Circulation

B) Compression

C) Consciousness

Q84: If a newborn is born with meconium stained amniotic fluid and is not breathing or has a heart rate below 100 beats per minute what intervention should be considered during resuscitation?

A) Administering epinephrine

B) Initiating chest compressions

C) Providing warmth and drying the baby

Q85: Which medication is used as a pain reliever for newborns undergoing certain medical procedures, such as circumcision?

A) Fentanyl

B) Morphine

C) Sucrose solution

Q86: What drug is commonly administered to newborns to stimulate breathing and improve lung function?

A) Albuterol

B) Atropine

C) Caffeine citrate

Q87: A newborn with jaundice receives phototherapy. What lab result indicates the effectiveness of phototherapy?

A) Decreased bilirubin levels

B) Elevated blood glucose levels

C) Increased liver enzyme levels

Q88: A newborn with suspected patent ductus arteriosus (PDA) is given indomethacin. What clinical sign suggests that the indomethacin therapy is effective?

A) Murmur intensity increases

B) Blood pressure decreases

C) PDA signs diminish

Q89: Which Apgar component assesses the newborn's reflex irritability or response to stimulation?

A) Pulse

B) Grimace

C) Color

Q90: A newborn receives the following Apgar scores: 7 at 1 minute and 9 at 5 minutes. What does this improvement in scores indicate?

A) The newborn's condition is deteriorating.

B) The newborn experienced a birth injury.

C) The newborn is responding well to interventions and stabilizing.

Q91: The "Four T's" are commonly used to identify the causes of postpartum hemorrhage. Which of the following is NOT one of the Four T's?

A) Tissue

B) Thrombin

C) Trauma

Q92: In cases of postpartum hemorrhage, if uterine massage and medications fail to control bleeding, what is the next step in management?

A) Immediate blood transfusion

B) Emergent hysterectomy

C) Administration of pain medication

Q93: The condition in which a blood clot forms within a deep vein is called:

A) Deep vein thrombosis DVT

B) Varicose veins

C) Superficial thrombophlebitis

Q94: Women who have undergone a cesarean birth and have additional possibility factors for thrombophlebitis may be given prophylactic treatment with:

A) Antibiotics

B) Analgesics

C) Blood thinners

Q95: Which of the following symptom requires immediate medical attention in a woman with thrombophlebitis?

A) Mild leg pain

B) Warmth and redness in the affected leg

C) Sudden chest pain and difficulty breathing

Q96: What is the recommended treatment for pulmonary embolism?

A) Administering pain medication

B) Bed rest and hydration

C) Anticoagulant therapy

Q97: Which of the following factors increases the possibility of developing pulmonary embolism in postpartum women?

A) Early ambulation after birth

B) Previous history of blood clots

C) Adequate fluid intake

Q98: The primary goal of treatment for DIC is to:

A) Increase platelet count

B) Prevent blood clot formation

C) Address the underlying cause and support blood clotting

Q99: Which of the following statements about DIC is true?

A) It is more common in the early stages of pregnancy.

B) It is a condition characterized by excessive blood clotting

C) It can lead to organ damage due to reduced blood flow

Q100: Which of the following symptoms may be observed in a woman with HELLP syndrome?

A) Increased platelet count

B) Severe headache and visual disturbances

C) Low blood pressure and reduced heart rate

Answer: B) Severe headache and visual disturbances

Q101: HELLP syndrome is most likely to occur during which trimester of pregnancy?

A) First trimester

B) Second trimester

C) Third trimester

Q102: Which population is at higher risk of developing hematoma after childbirth?

A) Primigravida's (first-time mothers)

B Women who have had a history of low platelet counts.

C) Mothers who had a cesarean section

Q103: What is the initial management for a suspected hematoma after childbirth?

A) Giving blood thinning medication.

B) Performing an emergency cesarean section

C) Assessing vital signs and notifying the healthcare provider

Q104: The most significant complication of a large postpartum hematoma is:

A) Infection at the site of the hematoma

B) Impaired blood flow to vital organs

C) Formation of blood clots in the legs

Q105: In the postpartum period, women with chronic hypertension should continue to be monitored for:

A) Gestational diabetes

B) Preeclampsia

C) Postpartum hemorrhage

Answer: B) Preeclampsia

Q106: Women with chronic hypertension should be advised to avoid certain over-the-counter medications during pregnancy, such as:

A) Iron supplements

B) Nonsteroidal anti-inflammatory drugs NSAIDs

C) Antacids

Q107: Chronic hypertension during pregnancy may increase the risk of developing what condition in the newborn?

A) Respiratory distress syndrome

B) Jaundice

C) Neural tube defects

Q108: What is the first-line management for gestational hypertension to reduce the risk of complications?

A) Bed rest and restricted activity

B) Antihypertensive medications

C) Increased intake of salt and fluids

Q109: Gestational hypertension may lead to what condition, which is characterized by the presence of protein in the urine?

A) Preeclampsia

B) Gestational diabetes

C) Placenta previa

Q110: Which of the following is a potential complication of magnesium sulfate administration?

A) Hyperglycemia

B) Hyperkalemia

C) Respiratory depression

Q111: When managing a woman with eclampsia, it is essential to monitor:

A) Fetal heart rate and uterine contractions

B) Maternal blood glucose levels

C) Maternal and fetal hemoglobin levels

Q112: Which of the following is a risk factor for developing postpartum endometritis?

A. Cesarean delivery

B. Full-term pregnancy

C. Exclusive breastfeeding

Q113: What is the recommended treatment for postpartum endometritis?

A. Intravenous antibiotics

B. Antipyretics only

C. No specific treatment needed

Q114: Which postpartum woman is at the highest risk for developing a wound infection?

A. A woman who had a vaginal delivery with an episiotomy

B. A woman who had a scheduled cesarean section without complications

C. A woman who had an emergency cesarean section due to fetal distress

Q115: To promote wound healing and prevent infection, the nurse should encourage the postpartum woman to:

A. Limit fluid intake to avoid excess urination

B. Keep the wound site open to air at all times

C. Practice good hand hygiene before and after wound care

Q116: Which statement indicates that the postpartum woman understands wound care after a cesarean section?

A. "I will apply hydrogen peroxide to the incision daily."

B. "I'll avoid using pillows to support my incision when sitting or lying down."

C. "I'll call my healthcare provider if I develop pain or tenderness at the incision site."

Q117: A postpartum woman with septic pelvic thrombophlebitis is at risk of developing which serious complication?

A. Preeclampsia

B. Pulmonary embolism

C. Gestational diabetes

Q118: Which nursing intervention is essential in caring for a postpartum woman with septic pelvic thrombophlebitis?

A. Encouraging frequent ambulation

B. Applying cold packs to the affected area

C. Monitoring vital signs and assessing for signs of sepsis

Q119: The postpartum woman with septic pelvic thrombophlebitis should be educated about:

A. The importance of early ambulation

B. The need for bed rest and immobilization

C. Potential complications and the importance of compliance with medication

Q120: Which nursing intervention is essential in caring for a postpartum woman with a urinary tract infection?

A. Encouraging fluid restriction to reduce urinary frequency

B. Promoting adequate fluid intake to flush out bacteria from the urinary tract

C. Applying a heating pad to the lower abdomen to relieve pain

Q121: A postpartum woman with a urinary tract infection asks the nurse about ways to prevent future infections. What should the nurse recommend?

A. Avoiding sexual intercourse

B. Maintaining proper perineal hygiene

C. Drinking large amounts of coffee and tea

Q122: Which complication can occur if a urinary tract infection is left untreated in the postpartum period?

A. Endometritis

B. Mastitis

C. Pyelonephritis

Q123: The nurse is caring for a newborn of a woman with diabetes. What should the nurse assess in the newborn to detect any potential complications related to maternal diabetes?

A. Abdominal circumference

B. Heart rate

C. Blood pressure

Q124: What is the most appropriate nursing intervention to prevent postpartum diabetes in a woman with gestational diabetes?

A. Providing glucose-rich snacks between meals

B. Promoting a sedentary lifestyle to conserve energy

C. Encouraging breastfeeding and skin to skin contact with the newborn

Q125: A postpartum woman is experiencing sleep disturbances and reports consuming alcohol before bedtime to help her sleep. What should the nurse educate the woman about regarding alcohol and sleep?

A. Alcohol consumption can improve sleep quality in the postpartum period.

B. Alcohol may initially induce sleep but disrupts the later stages of sleep, leading to poorer sleep quality.

C. Alcohol has no effect on sleep patterns or can be safely used to aid sleep.

Q126: A postpartum woman with sleep disturbances is concerned about the safety of taking sleep medications while breastfeeding. What should the nurse recommend?

A. Over-the-counter sleep medications are safe to use while breastfeeding.

B. The woman should avoid all sleep medications to ensure the baby's safety during breastfeeding.

C. The woman should consult her healthcare provider to discuss safe sleep medication options while breastfeeding.

Q127: What is the best nursing intervention for a postpartum woman experiencing sleep disturbances and postpartum depression?

A. Provide emotional support and encourage open communication about her feelings.

B. Administer sleep medications as prescribed to ensure adequate rest.

C. Encourage the woman to isolate herself to avoid overwhelming situations.

Q128: The nurse is assessing a postpartum woman for postpartum depression. Which assessment tool is commonly used to screen for postpartum mood disorders?

A. Edinburgh Postnatal Depression Scale (EPDS)

B. Mini-Mental State Examination MMSE

C. Geriatric Depression Scale (GDS)

Q129: The nurse is caring for a woman with postpartum psychosis. What is the priority nursing intervention?

A. Encouraging the woman to rest and sleep as much as possible

B. Providing a safe environment and close observation

C. Administering antidepressant medication as prescribed

Q130: A postpartum woman with postpartum depression expresses thoughts of harming herself and her infant. What is the appropriate nursing action?

A. Encourage the woman to talk openly about her feelings.

B. Inform the woman's partner or support person and healthcare provider immediately.

C. Reassure the woman that these thoughts are common and will pass with time.

Q131: The nurse is preparing a discharge plan for a postpartum woman with substance abuse issues. What components need to be part of the plan?

A. Referral to a lactation consultant for breastfeeding support

B. Arrangement of outpatient substance abuse treatment

C. Recommendation of herbal supplements to aid recovery

Q132: A postpartum woman admits to using illicit drugs during pregnancy and expresses guilt and concern about her baby's health. How should the nurse respond?

A. Dismiss the woman's feelings to avoid causing further distress.

B. Reassure the woman that the baby will likely be unaffected by the drug use.

C. Offer nonjudgmental support and encourage open communication about her concerns.

Q133: The nurse is assessing a newborn with suspected cyanotic heart disease. Which assessment finding would support this diagnosis?

A. Normal heart rate and respiratory rate

B. Cyanosis that worsens with crying or feeding

C. Absence of any heart murmurs

Q134: Which cyanotic heart defect involves the presence of four anomalies: ventricular septal defect, overriding aorta, pulmonary stenosis, and right ventricular hypertrophy?

A. Coarctation of the aorta (CoA)

B. Atrial septal defect (ASD)

C. Tetralogy of Fallot (TOF)

Q135: When caring for a newborn with cyanotic heart disease, what nursing intervention should be prioritized to promote oxygenation?

A. Encouraging deep breaths and coughing exercises

B. Positioning the infant in a supine position

C. Providing cluster care to minimize disturbances

Q136: Which a cyanotic heart disease involves a narrowing of the aorta leading to increased blood pressure in the upper extremities or decreased blood pressure in the lower extremities?

A. Tetralogy of Fallot (TOF)

B. Patent ductus arteriosus (PDA)

C. Coarctation of the aorta (CoA)

Q137: A term newborn experiences an apneic episode with bradycardia and cyanosis. Which condition should the nurse suspect as the cause of this event?

A. Patent ductus arteriosus (PDA)

B. Transient tachypnea of the newborn (TTN)

C. Meconium aspiration syndrome (MAS)

Q138: Which maternal condition is most strongly associated with an increased risk of the newborn developing Transient Tachypnea of the Newborn?

A. Gestational diabetes

B. Preeclampsia

C. Maternal asthma

Q139: A preterm infant is at a higher possibility of developing pneumothorax compared to a full-term infant. Which of the following factors contributes to this increased possibility in preterm neonates?

A The lungs produce more surfactant at higher levels.

B. Weaker intercostal muscles and rib cage

C. Delayed closure of the ductus arteriosus

Q140: A newborn with suspected meconium aspiration is showing respiratory distress, cyanosis, and decreased breath sounds on the right side of the chest. What is the most appropriate initial intervention for this neonate?

A. Administering intravenous antibiotics

B. Performing chest physiotherapy to clear the meconium

C. Providing oxygen therapy and respiratory support

Q141: A preterm newborn is diagnosed with hypoxic-ischemic encephalopathy (HIE) and is at risk of developing seizures. Which of the following is the most appropriate medication for the prevention of seizures in this neonate?

A. Diazepam

B. Phenobarbital

C. Fentanyl

Q142: A preterm newborn is experiencing tremors and irritability shortly after birth. The baby is mother has a history of substance abuse. What is the probable reason for these symptoms?

A. Hypocalcemia

B. Hypoglycemia

C. Hypomagnesemia

Q143: A newborn is diagnosed with a grade III intraventricular hemorrhage. Which of the following clinical manifestations would the nurse expect to observe in the baby?

A. Hypotonia and poor feeding

B. Cyanosis and tachypnea

C. Hyperactivity and jitteriness

Q144: A pregnant woman in her first trimester visits the clinic for a routine check-up. The nurse is reviewing her medical history and notes that she had a previous pregnancy affected by a neural tube defect. What intervention should the nurse recommend to reduce the risk of recurrence?

A. Initiate genetic testing to determine if the NTD is hereditary.

B. Prescribe high doses of vitamin D supplementation.

C. Administer folic acid supplements in higher doses than usual.

Q145: A newborn is born to a mother who has a history of alcohol abuse. The infant is showing signs of fetal alcohol syndrome FAS. What physical features might the nurse expect to find in the newborn?

A. Microcephaly, smooth philtrum, and thin upper lip.

B. Large birth weight and hyperactivity.

C. Absence of palmar creases and low muscle tone.

Q146: A neonate is born with an abdominal wall defect that allows the abdominal organs to protrude outside the body. What is the appropriate nursing care for this newborn immediately after birth?

A. Applying a sterile dressing to cover the defect.

B. Administering a lumbar puncture to assess for infection.

C. Encouraging breastfeeding to promote wound healing.

Q147: A newborn is diagnosed with biliary atresia. The nurse knows that this condition involves the obstruction or absence of which structure?

A. Gallbladder

B. Liver lobes

C. Common bile duct

Q148: A term newborn is diagnosed with iron-deficiency anemia. The nurse is providing education to the parents about iron-rich foods. Which food item would be most appropriate to recommend to the parents?

A. Honey

B. Cow's milk

C. Pureed spinach

Q149: A term newborn is exclusively breastfed and does not receive a vitamin K injection at birth. The nurse educates the parents about the signs and symptoms of vitamin K deficiency bleeding. Which bleeding site is commonly associated with late-onset vitamin K deficiency bleeding?

A. Skin

B. Gastrointestinal tract

C. Respiratory system

Q150: A neonate born to a mother on long-term anticonvulsant therapy is at risk for vitamin K deficiency. Which mechanism explains the increased risk of vitamin K deficiency in this newborn?

A. Impaired vitamin K synthesis in the liver

B. Enhanced vitamin K absorption in the intestines

C. Decreased vitamin K excretion through the kidneys

Q151: A nurse is educating new parents about neonatal jaundice and hyperbilirubinemia. The parents ask if there are any preventive measures, they can take to reduce the risk of their baby developing jaundice. What should the nurse recommend?

A. Limiting the newborn's fluid intake

B. Frequent exposure to direct sunlight

C. Ensuring adequate breastfeeding or formula feeding

Q152: A baby with ABO incompatibility is experiencing severe hyperbilirubinemia, and phototherapy is not effective in reducing bilirubin levels. What additional treatment modality may be considered in this situation?

A. Exchange transfusion

B. Antibiotic therapy

C. Oxygen supplementation

Q153: A pregnant woman with blood type B has just given birth to a baby with blood type A. The baby is at risk for ABO incompatibility. What nursing intervention can help prevent complications in this situation?

A. Encouraging early breastfeeding

B. Administering intramuscular iron supplements

C. Monitoring the baby's temperature every hour

Q154: A pregnant woman with Rh-negative blood type is at risk for developing antibodies against Rh-positive blood. What intervention during pregnancy can help prevent Rh sensitization in the mother?

A. Administering Rh immunoglobulin (Rig) at 28 weeks of gestation

B. Initiating iron supplementation to improve hemoglobin levels

C. Monitoring blood pressure regularly for signs of preeclampsia

Q155: A neonate with G6PD deficiency experiences a hemolytic crisis. What intervention should the nurse expect to be prescribed to manage this crisis effectively?

A. Administering iron supplements

B. Providing phototherapy for jaundice

C. Avoiding triggers and supportive care

Q156: G6PD deficiency is more common in certain ethnic groups. Which of the following ethnic groups has a higher incidence of G6PD deficiency?

A. Caucasian

B. African-American

C. Asian

Q157: Due to thicker blood and slow blood flow caused by polycythemia, what clinical signs might be seen in a newborn?

A. Petechiae and purpura on the skin

B. Poor feeding and lethargy

C. Hyperactivity and irritability

Q158: A neonate is at risk of polycythemia due to delayed cord clamping during birth. In which situation is delayed cord clamping typically practiced?

A. Neonates born with meconium-stained amniotic fluid

B. Neonates requiring immediate resuscitation

C. Neonates born preterm

Q159: Hyper viscosity can result in impaired blood flow and oxygen delivery to tissues. Which of the following clinical manifestations may be observed in a neonate with hyper viscosity due to decreased tissue perfusion?

A. Cyanosis and tachycardia

B. Bradycardia and hypotension

C. Hyperactivity and irritability

Q160: A neonate born to a mother with gestational thrombocytopenia is at risk of developing the same condition. What is the most common cause of gestational thrombocytopenia?

A. Autoimmune disorder

B. Bacterial infection

C. Physiologic response to pregnancy

Q161: The maternal nurse is educating new parents about preventing neonatal sepsis. Which measure's most effective in reducing the risk of sepsis in newborns?

A. Avoiding routine handwashing

B. Delaying vaccination schedule

C. Ensuring proper umbilical cord care

Q162: A newborn is suspected to have a congenital bacterial infection. Besides the complete blood count (CBC) and differential, which additional laboratory test should be performed to guide appropriate antibiotic therapy?

A. C-reactive protein (CRP)

B. Thyroid-stimulating hormone TSH

C. Blood glucose level

Q163: A neonate is born to a mother with untreated syphilis infection. Which component of the complete blood count (CBC) and differential is essential to monitor in the newborn to identify potential complications related to syphilis infection?

A. Hemoglobin (Hb) level

B. White Blood Cell (WBC) count

C. Platelet count

Q164: After a lumbar puncture, the neonate develops a fever and becomes irritable. The maternal nurse notices increased resistance in neck flexion (nuchal rigidity). What is the probable reason for these symptoms?

A. Normal reaction to the procedure

B. Allergic reaction to the local anesthetic

C. Possible meningitis or infection

Q165: Before performing a lumbar puncture on a neonate, the healthcare provider should ensure that the baby's fontanelles are:

A. Closed

B. Pulsating

C. Depressed

Q166: A newborn is born with microcephaly intracranial calcifications or other congenital anomalies. The maternal nurse suspects a viral infection during pregnancy. Which virus is most likely responsible for these findings?

A. Zika virus

B. Herpes simplex virus (HSV)

C. The human immunodeficiency virus HIV.

Q167: A breastfeeding mother is diagnosed with syphilis. The maternal nurse provides education on preventing transmission to the newborn What is the most suitable advice among the options provided?

A. Avoid breastfeeding until treatment is completed.

B. Continue breastfeeding but use nipple shields.

C. Express breast milk and discard it until treatment is completed.

Q168: A pregnant woman with a history of genital herpes has a vaginal outbreak close to her due date. The maternal nurse discusses the management plan to reduce neonatal transmission. Which intervention is most appropriate?

A. Administer intravenous acyclovir during labor and delivery.

B. Perform a cesarean section (C-section) before the outbreak resolves.

C. Administer oral antibiotics to the newborn immediately after birth.

Q169: A neonate is born with a suspected fungal infection, and an antifungal medication is prescribed. Which nursing action is essential when administering intravenous antifungal medications to neonates?

A. Administering the medication as a rapid intravenous bolus.

B. Monitoring for signs of cardiac dysrhythmias during administration.

C. Avoiding intravenous fluids to prevent medication dilution.

Q170: A neonate is diagnosed with congenital herpes infection. The maternal nurse educates the parents about the importance of antiviral therapy. Which statement by the parents indicates an understanding of the education provided?

A. "The antiviral medication will cure the infection completely."

B. "The antiviral medication will only help with symptom relief."

C. "The antiviral medication will reduce the severity and duration of the infection."

Q171: A neonate is diagnosed with a genetic disorder affecting gluconeogenesis, resulting in recurrent episodes of hypoglycemia. Which of the following measures is essential for managing hypoglycemic episodes in this neonate?

A. Providing high-carbohydrate formula feeds

B. Administering intravenous insulin

C. Offering regular feeds with a balance of carbohydrates, proteins, and fats

Q172: A neonate is born with an inborn error of metabolism that affects the metabolism of long-chain fatty acids. The nurse should closely monitor the neonate for which potential complication related to this condition?

A. Hypoglycemia

B. Hyperbilirubinemia

C. Respiratory distress

Q173: A family has a history of Marfa syndrome, an autosomal dominant disorder. If one parent has Marfa syndrome, what is the chance of their child inheriting the disease?

A. 25%

B. 50%

C. 75%

Q174: A newborn is born to a mother with pregestational diabetes. The baby is large for gestational age, and the mother had an uneventful pregnancy. The infant is at risk for a specific birth injury due to macrosomia. What is the potential birth injury associated with macrosomia in infants of diabetic mothers?

A. Brachial plexus injury

B. Clavicle fracture

C. Hip dislocation

Q175: A newborn is at risk for hypoglycemia due to maternal diabetes during pregnancy. The nurse is monitoring the baby's blood glucose levels and observes a reading below the normal range. What should the nurse do as the initial intervention for this newborn?

A. Administer IV dextrose solution

B. Offer formula feeding to the baby

C. Encourage the mother to breastfeed the baby

Test 7 Answer Key

1	C	27	B	53	C
2	B	28	B	54	C
3	C	29	C	55	B
4	C	30	A	56	B
5	C	31	C	57	C
6	C	32	B	58	B
7	A	33	A	59	B
8	B	34	A	60	A
9	A	35	B	61	A
10	C	36	B	62	B
11	C	37	B	63	C
12	C	38	B	64	C
13	A	39	C	65	C
14	B	40	A	66	B
15	A	41	C	67	A
16	A	42	B	68	C
17	C	43	B	69	C
18	C	44	C	70	C
19	B	45	A	71	A
20	A	46	B	72	C
21	B	47	B	73	C
22	C	48	B	74	A
23	B	49	C	75	A
24	C	50	C	76	B
25	B	51	C	77	A
26	B	52	C	78	B

79	A	106	B	133	B
80	B	107	B	134	C
81	C	108	A	135	C
82	B	109	A	136	C
83	A	110	C	137	C
84	C	111	A	138	B
85	C	112	A	139	B
86	C	113	A	140	C
87	A	114	C	141	B
88	C	115	C	142	C
89	B	116	C	143	A
90	C	117	B	144	C
91	B	118	C	145	A
92	B	119	C	146	A
93	A	120	B	147	C
94	C	121	B	148	C
95	C	122	C	149	B
96	C	123	A	150	A
97	B	124	C	151	C
98	C	125	B	152	A
99	C	126	C	153	A
100	B	127	A	154	A
101	C	128	A	155	C
102	C	129	B	156	C
103	C	130	B	157	B
104	B	131	B	158	A
105	B	132	C	159	A

160	C	166	A	172	A
161	C	167	A	173	B
162	A	168	B	174	A
163	C	169	B	175	C
164	C	170	C		
165	A	171	C		